The World Is:
A Metatext on our Place

Jake DeBacher

Lumbering Tom Press

ISBN: 0615981976
ISBN-13: 978-0615981970

CONTENTS

INTRODUCTION I.

What you'll find in this book are a series of passages that state, figuratively or analytically, what the world is. There is a full page of text for each entry, but the statement is set apart from the background. Collecting these statements started as a folly but soon enough evolved into something bordering on mania—how have the best minds of human history characterized our collective frame of existence? Are such characterizations acts of reduction, or artifacts of self-actualized understanding? If that's the case, is it possible for that understanding to be transferred to another person? Alternatively, what breed of madness leads a person to believe he can make such vast statements? These were the questions that drove me into the millions of digitized books available in public domain.

Whatever answers there are to be had to the above questions, if any, are not immediately self-evident—only fitting, I suppose, for a topic so vast. Accompanying this dearth of obvious answers is an abundance of intellectual pitfalls. As we can see in a shockingly astute 1903 essay by the physician Herman Gasser (the largely forgotten father of Nobel laureate Herbert S. Gasser) — "Our idea of the world is not the world's system." This sounds like a truism, but it illustrates a principle that is essential in a text such as this. As any cocky student of object oriented ontology will tell you, our conceptualizations have impact on the material world only insofar as they can drive our actions. But our ideas about the world *do*, in a sense, establish *our* system—our functional world as we perceive it.

As mentioned above, there are two types of selections within: *analytic-descriptive* and *figurative*. The former is a self-explanatory category, but that's not to say that those statements are unimportant or unworthy of critical thought. The author is taking a step beyond what would be the "ordinary" enormity of a statement regarding "all the inhabitants of the world" or even "all the matter in the world"—and rather chooses (one can only assume intentionally, or at least subconsciously, or at least not *entirely* unthinkingly) choosing to speak on the highest magnitude possible, equating the world with its inhabitants. The ultimate metonymy.

Let me give an example. Luzhin's observation in *Crime and Punishment* that "science says, 'Love thyself above all, because **everything in the world is founded on self-interest**'" is inadequate because he doesn't take that final, important step into true metonymy. Meanwhile, when Father Zosima in *The Brothers Karamazov* claims that the masses "maintain that **the world is getting more and more united, more and more bound**

together in brotherly community, as it overcomes distance and sets thoughts flying through the air," he dialectically rests the worth of the world on the shoulders of its inhabitants. It seems at first an arbitrary division, but it's important—at least, it is for me—that the author have enough faith in his analogy to fully equate the category of earth's inhabitants with the earth itself. Implicit in the statement is that the value of the world *is* the value of its inhabitants.

On the other hand are the *figurative* statements. Like the analytic statements, all of the figurative statements within are absolute in their conflation of the world and its inhabitants, but here there is a bit more room for authorial freedom. The noteworthy difference from the analytic statements is that all of the figurative statements are, by definition, self-effacing. Once the analogy has been presented—the world as a bad dog (Joseph Conrad), an old woman (Thomas Carlyle), a wooden tiger (Tukaram)—it is conceptualized and for a moment unconsciously factualized by the reader, and then shunted away by our minds in their ultimate function as binary machines which analyze observations as factual or not. We're left then with just that ghost of a feeling, the memory of a visceral sensation (of having *known*) which leaves only the faintest imprint on the subjective lens between our binary machine and all that's *out there*. Incidentally, that imprint is the same vital energy that sustains poetry. "I do not think anybody ever knows... the discreet handling of metaphor, unless he has been properly educated in poetry," Robert Frost told a group of Amherst students in 1931.

One might say, then, that these momentary fictions actually serve as the ultimate foundation for thought. As we develop from an existence of undifferentiated overstimulation, we create schemata as subjective modes of control over and understanding of objects. In this view, metaphors are manipulations of schemata. A poet with superb grasp of metaphor might be said to hold singular grasp over his schemata, while a person who dismisses poetry in favor of, say, *The Bachelor* is actually slave to his own proto-schemata. Further, this position would maintain that metaphors and other non-concrete thinking hold (or for the metaphysically reckless, *are*) the essence of existence. Our separation from objects only extends as far as our metaphysical thinking, which by this reasoning rests squarely on metaphor.

And here we might have a whiff of an answer to one of the questions posed above: what is there to be found in the statements of the next hundred-odd pages—the reflection of ultimate understanding, or only ultimate arrogance? At the very least, here there is the *possibility* of a really exceptional wisdom. And that's an awfully exciting thing! Reading some of these passages is a little like witnessing a moment of someone else's inspiration: you don't need to share the insight to marvel at its majesty, perhaps even feel a bit envious of the author's hubris. And that indefiniteness, the *possibility*, is the last quality of the metaphor that I'll mention here. Analogies are by definition provisional, functional only in particular circumstances, meant to have some utility, no matter how indirect. To achieve this usefulness they need only to *suggest* truths, not *be* truths. This is another paradox—they are simultaneously reductive *and* expansive, opening another avenue for our understanding and interpretation of the world and our relationship to it.

Although I slightly mocked the object oriented ontologists a little earlier, I would like to borrow a phrase from one. In his introduction to *Realist Magic: Objects, Ontology, Causality* (available for free from the wonderful Open Humanities Press), Timothy Morton refers to the essential core of all objects as "an open secret," following the idea that "at this very moment, this very object, as an intrinsic aspect of its being, is incapable of being anything else." Perhaps that is in some way what we see in the pages that follow. Here are over a hundred authors that have consciously examined the fragmented lens developed over their lives through uncountable interactions with objects as well as figurative interpretations, and set down a crystallization of the biggest subject that a person could conceivably reduce: the world. And in doing so they give you, if you will allow them, a momentary freedom from the literal, and contribute a minute addition to your own singularly vast schema. This is a collection of open secrets.

INTRODUCTION II.

Or, conceivably, that's all just foolish semiotic idealism. Sweeping statements with no foundation on the concrete, I learned in middle-school English, are crutches for the weak-minded. A case in point: one of the works I draw material from, Elizabeth Elton Smith's *The Three Eras of Woman's Life* (1835), provided six "world-is" statements—and, if I'd stretched the definition, could have yielded several more. Is this merely the ultimate indefinition? Is she so incapable of finding the proper noun, of locating the specificity that gives words meaning? Is she actually *devaluing* language by lapsing so frequently into grand metonymy? After all, it's difficult to critique her work if all of its components are phrased in immeasurable abstractions.

That may, in fact, be the case. The linguistic tools available to any good writer are no less available to weak writers, but they cannot be expected to provide the same results for both groups. I have no particular desire to denigrate what I've spent so much time collecting and pondering, but it would have been impossible (not to mention worrisome) if, in all that time, I hadn't at least considered the possibility that everything herein is of no great importance.

So, granting for a moment that these may not be profound crystallizations of actualized minds, this book is clearly filled with *something* that could be worth reading—what?

Starting with the most patently obvious, there probably aren't a whole lot of collections of unrelated passages spanning fourteen centuries to be found. The fact remains that there can't be much demand for such collections, but that's not to say that there aren't some real gems to be found nonetheless. The works reprinted here are cut off at 1924 to avoid copyright issues, but I hope that that only hobbles rather than entirely incapacitates the viability of the scope of selections. I drew on a number of magazines that that republished content collected from international journals and newspapers (much like *Reader's Digest*, though many of these magazines predate the venerable American rag by more than a century) which are endless sources of amusement, as they no doubt were for their original readers. There are a variety of sermons and religious pamphlets, as religious-types are predisposed to making universalizing statements. There is a bit of a play by William Burnaby, the 17th-century translator of the *Satyricon*; a handful of poems by the Bhakti mystic Tukaram; a passage of St. Augustine's immense and terrifying *The City of God*; and a smattering of more familiar names (Kant, Emerson, Conrad...).

And in defense to the public-domain-imposed limit on breadth, there is at least the redeeming fact that all of the books excerpted can be accessed for free on Google Books (and it's worth mentioning that that fact made this collection feasible in the first place). If something piques your interest, go and find it. There are dozens of websites and blogs dedicated to forgotten texts, but with hundreds of books being newly digitized each day, there are worlds far beyond what I turned up, yet to be explored.

It's probably bad form to struggle to find utility as justification for what is essentially a creative work, but the fact of the matter is that I truly don't know if the depth of this project extends past shallow frivolity. I feel sure that a part of the project's value was in continuing to work at it long past my first waves of doubt, through unanswered questions, and, while I have no idea if that benefit can transfer through to a casual reader or a curious peruser—not, I suppose, unlike witnessing inspiration from afar—I actively hope it can.

It's hard to imagine that there's some particular intellectual poverty beyond my own that this collection could relieve, but perhaps I'm wrong about that. Even apart from my role as the collector, there's a peculiar self-indulgence built into each statement here that ought to speak to every thinking being: the notion that, no matter how hard we fight to divorce ourselves from anthropocentrism, the greatness of the world is only *potential* until actualized by its inhabitants. H. G. Wells spoke on this theme in 1902, just a few syntactic choices away from meriting inclusion in this book's body:

> …some day this earth of ours, tideless and slow moving, will be dead and frozen, and all that has lived upon it will be frozen and done with. There surely man must end. That of all such nightmares is the most insistently convincing.
>
> And yet one doesn't believe it.
>
> At least I do not. And I do not believe in these things because I have come to believe in certain other things,—in the coherency and purpose in the world and in the greatness of human destiny. Worlds may freeze and suns may perish, but there stirs something within us now that can never die again.

That is, in part, what these passages speak to. When we characterize the world, it is, explicitly or not, always an extension of our relation to it. That's why the prototypical earth seized by early environmentalists was personified as a *mother*: our understanding of it is contingent on our understanding of ourselves as characters integral to its importance.

As to whether or not that tendency is "correct," Hamlet proposes an answer: "There are more things in heaven and earth, Horatio, than are dreamt of in your philosophy." But this book is not for correcting that bias, but rather for reveling in it. We *are* in this world—it's the literal frame of our existence—and it's worth acknowledging and analyzing that. So with only the slight guilt of indulgence in an intrinsic bias, here's a collection of existential revelry.

Jake DeBacher

March 2014

1.

THE WORLD IS A SOCIAL PLACE

conversation (which took place as the coach rolled along lazily by the river side) that though Miss Rebecca Sharp has twice had occasion to thank Heaven, it has been, in the first place, for ridding her of some person whom she hated, and secondly, for enabling her to bring her enemies to some sort of perplexity or confusion; neither of which are very amiable motives for religious gratitude, or such as would be put forward by persons of a kind and placable disposition. Miss Rebecca was not, then, in the least kind or placable. All the world used her ill, said this young misanthropist, and we may be pretty certain that persons whom all the world treats ill, deserve entirely the treatment they get. The world is a looking-glass, and gives back to every man the reflection of his own face. Frown at it, and it will in turn look sourly upon you; laugh at it and with it, and it is a jolly kind companion; and so let all young persons take their choice. This is certain, that if the world neglected Miss Sharp, she never was known to have done a good action in behalf of anybody; nor can it be expected that twenty-four young ladies should all be as amiable as the heroine of this work, Miss Sedley (whom we have selected for the very reason that she was the bestnatured of all, otherwise what on earth' was to have prevented us from putting up Miss Swartz, or Miss Crump, or Miss Hopkins, as heroine in her place ?) —it could not be expected that every one should be of the humble and gentle temper of Miss Amelia Sedley; should take every opportunity to vanquish Rebecca's hard-heartedness and ill-humour; and, by a thousand kind words and

Joseph Conrad – *Victory* (1915)

"She was engaged in the task of defending her position in life," said Heyst. "It's a very respectable task."

""Is that it? I had some idea it was that," confessed Davidson.

He then imparted to Heyst the story of the violent proceedings following on the discovery of his flight. Heyst's polite attention to the tale took on a sombre cast; but he manifested no surprise, and offered no comment. When Davidson had finished he handed down the shawl into the boat, and Davidson promised to do his best to return it to Mrs. Schomberg in some secret fashion. Heyst expressed his thanks in a few simple words, set off by his manner of finished courtesy. Davidson prepared to depart. They were not looking at each other. Suddenly Heyst spoke:

"You understand that this was a case of odious persecution, don't you? I became aware of it and—"

It was a view which the sympathetic Davidson was capable of appreciating.

"I am not surprised to hear it," he said placidly. "Odious enough, I dare say. And you, of course—not being a married man —were free to step in. Ah, well!"

He sat down in the stern-sheets, and already had the steering lines in his hands when Heyst observed abruptly:

"The world is a bad dog. It will bite you if you give it a chance; but I think that here we can safely defy the fates."

When relating all this to me, Davidson's only comment was:

"Funny notion of defying the fates — to take a woman in tow!"

Sir Test. How do ye spend your time?

Saunt. At *Will's* Coffee-house, and waiting on the Ladies.

Sir Test. Then you're a Wit too?

Saunt. A piece of one—.

Gripe. (*Aside*) A half one he means—

Saunt. I write Songs to the Fair; all my Amusements are dedicated to the Ladies: for I have no Muse but my Mistress.

Sir Test. A pretty Life! then you never have any thing to do?

Saunt. O never, Sir, the World is like a Ship where the inferiour Wretches guide the Vessel, order the Sails, and handle the dirty Ropes, while Gentlemen are the Passengers that have no business but only to look on.

For we have Wit enough we ne're imploy it,
Let others rule the World while we enjoy it.

Sir Test. (*Aside*) Here's a Rogue! Do ye never Study Sir?

Saunt. In a Morning while my Man is drawing on my Shoes,—I just look into Books, but never go so far as to know any thing of 'em; a Gentleman should only have a Tast of every thing.

Sir Test. And know nothing! well Sir, what other powerful reasons have you to make me match into your Family?

Saunt. None so great as my Family it self, Sir, 'tis as ancient as any in *England*; the *Saunters* were before the Conqueror, and a good Family is better than Riches, besides Sir, I'm one of the old East-India Company, and no Man living knows what I'm worthy.

Sir Test. Your unkown Estates are commonly none at all, and as

Charles William Day – *The Maxims, Experiences, and Observations of Agogos* (1844)

Knowledge of the world depends on the power of drawing general inferences from individual examples; and he is the most likely to be correct who has the greatest number of facts at his command.

The world is a mongrel, — half spaniel, half wolf. Lash it often, and, when you require it, a whistle will bring it to your feet : show but the slightest symptom of fear, and it will turn round upon, and worry you, even unto the death.

Satire is a prompt recipe for making bitter enemies; and the deadliest of all schisms is that created by a witticism.

If you would thrive in the world, pretend to take people at the value they set upon themselves, which may be enormous, rather than at their real worth, which may be — nothing.

The world stamps "Innocent" on the bold front of the successful plunderer, whilst the silent despair of the victim ruined in asserting his rights, is but too often received as evidence of a guilty attempt at extortion.

Look less at an opinion given, than at the character of him who pronounces it. Incalculable mischief is often done by people unreflectingly receiving as " authority " the opinions of a mere ass, on subjects with which they are imperfectly acquainted, but on which he is supposed to be better informed, yet which are often the farthest from the truth, the judgment of such a person being either swayed by the most absurd prejudices, or blinded by the most foul am apt to see clear through a subject, where the penetration of ordinary people extends but half way, there is no fact more simple and manifest, than that the death of a great man is a matter of very little importance. Much as we may think of ourselves, and much as we may excite the empty plaudits of the million, it is certain that the greatest among us do actually fill but an exceeding small space in the world ; and it is equally certain, that even that small space is quickly supplied when we leave it vacant. "Of what consequence is it," said the elegant Pliny, "that individuals appear, or make their exit? —**the world is a theatre whose scenes and actors are continually changing.**" Never did philosopher speak more correctly, and I only wonder, that so wise a remark could have existed so many ages, and mankind not have laid it more to heart. Sage follows on in the footsteps of sage; one hero just steps out of his triumphal car, to make way for the hero who comes after him ; and of the proudest monarch it is merely said, that — "he slept with his fathers, and his successors reigned in his stead."

The world, to tell the private truth, cares but little for their loss, and if left to itself would soon forget to grieve; and though a nation has often been figuratively drowned in tears on the death of a great man, yet it is ten chances to one if an individual tear has been shed on the occasion, excepting from the forlorn pen of some hungry author. It is the historian, the biographer, and the poet, who have the whole burthen of grief to sustain — who, kind souls! like undertakers in England, act the part of chief mourners—who

"Nora, the good beast. Last night, when all that was going on, those miserable fellows gave her something—most like some sort of fungus roasted with suet. She's dying now."

"Where is she?"

"Before the kennel."

Sonnenkamp went with the keeper to the enclosure where the dogs were kept. There lay Nora, with her loosened chain beside her.

"Nora!" cried Sonnenkamp. The dog wagged its tail, raised its head, blinked, dropped its head and died.

There was a mournful look in the dog's eyes. Sonnenkamp seemed to like to torment himself with it, he looked so steadily at it.

"Bury the dog before Roland notices it," he said, at last.

"Where shall we bury it ?"

"By the ash. Skin her, though; her skin is worth money."

"No, Sir ; I can't do that. I loved the dog too much to skin her."

"Very well; then bury her with her skin on."

He went away, and for a long time wandered about in the garden; and at last could not withstand the temptation of going to the spot where the dog was buried.

"Yes," he said to himself, aloud; "so it is. The fungus roasted in fat represents the world. **The world is a fungus roasted in fat. It tastes good, but it poisons!"**

He returned to the house.

The dogs were howling dolefully, as if they knew that a

Musick, *Literature*, and *Science*; each of which branches off into numerous subdivisions, set forth in a copious Table of Contents. The articles in general are as entertaining as those in the "Philosophy of Nature;" but they bear evident marks of that *sombre* turn of thought alluded to in our last.

We take as an example:

> "The miseries of those who have no ties of friendship or affection.
>
> "Whatever be his rank, his wealth, or his ability, no one can be esteemed fortunate, who has no ties of friendship, of blood, or of humanity, to chain him to existence. He creeps upon the earth as a worm! The sun sets, the evening star rises, flowers expand, and the autumnal moon lulls all nature; but to him every joy is in perspective, his bosom is void, and his heart is cheerless—for no one hails him as a friend, and no one regards him as a brother, or benefactor.

—Well and often has it been said that **the world is a wilderness to him who is destitute of a friend**. A wilderness, too, not of flowers or of plants, of rocks and of mountains, wild, yet not remote from beauty or sublimity; but a wilderness of weeds, or a sterile, parched, and burning desert. In the deepest recess of Nature, he, on the contrary, who feels the fine impulses of the heart, wanders not alone. In the midst of a Court, the Statesman nauseates the smile and the whisper, which invade him, unless his heart acknowledges to his judgment, that his glory is not wanting in the applause of his want of knowledge of the persons he addresses,—until he finds that he is the complement of his hearers;—that they drink his words because he fulfils for them their own nature; the deeper he dives into his privatest, secretest presentiment, to his wonder he finds, this is the most acceptable, most public, and universally true. The people delight in it; the better part of every man feels, This is my music; this is myself.

In self-trust, all the virtues are comprehended. Free should the scholar be,—free and brave. Free even to the definition of freedom, "without any hindrance that does not arise out of his own constitution." Brave; for fear is a thing, which a scholar by his very function puts behind him. Fear always springs from ignorance. It is a shame to him if his tranquility, amid dangerous times, arise from the presumption, that, like children and women, his is a protected class; or if he seek a temporary peace by the diversion of his bushes, peeping into microscopes, and turning rhymes, as a boy whistles to keep his courage up. So is the danger a danger still; so is the fear worse. Manlike let him turn and face it. Let him look into its eye and search its nature, inspect its origin,—see the whelping of this lion,—which lies no great way back; he will then find in himself a perfect comprehension of its nature and extent; he will have made his friends meet on the other side, and can henceforth defy it, and pass on superior. **The world is his, who can see through its pretension.** What deafness, what stone-blind custom, what overgrown error you behold, is there only by sufferance,—by your gain in my profession; a principle, if I mistake not, pretty general and pretty powerful in the present day. 3dly. I hope the public will consider that I have been a timorous man, or, if you will, a coward, from my youth, so that I cannot fight — my belly is so big that I cannot run — and I am so great a lover of eating and drinking that I cannot starve. When those three things are considered, I hope they will fully account for my past conduct, and procure me the liberty of going on in the same *uniform* tenor for the future. No just judgment can be formed of a man's character and conduct unless every circumstance is taken in and fairly attended to ; I therefore hope that this justice will be done in my case. I am also verily pursuaded that if all those who are cowards as well as myself, but who are better off in other respects, and therefore can and do run whenever danger is near them, would befriend me, I should have no inconsiderable body on my side. Peace be with the Congress and the army; I mean no reflections; but **the world is a wide field**, and I wish everybody would do as they would be done by. Finally, I do hereby recant, draw back, eat in, and swallow down, every word that I have ever spoken, writ ten or printed to the prejudice of the United States of America, hoping it will not only satisfy the good people in general, but also all those scatter-brained fellows, who call one another out to shoot pistols in the air, while they tremble so much they cannot hit the mark. In the mean time I will return to labor with assiduity in my lawful calling, and essays and intelligence as before shall be gratefully accepted by the Public's (as he would of course), he might fall in love with Kate, who would be keeping my house, and—and—marry her, eh! uncle? Who knows?"

"Who, indeed!" snarled Ralph.

"How happy we should be!" cried Nicholas with enthusiasm. "The pain of parting is nothing to the joy of meeting again. Kate will be a beautiful woman, and I so proud to hear them say so, and mother so happy to be with us once again, and all these sad times forgotten, and—" The picture was too bright a one to bear, and Nicholas, fairly overpowered by it, smiled faintly, and burst into tears.

This simple family, born and bred in retirement, and wholly unacquainted with what is called **the world—a conventional phrase which, being interpreted, signifieth all the rascals in it**—mingled their tears together at the thought of their first separation; and, this first gush of feeling over, were proceeding to dilate with all the buoyancy of untried hope on the bright prospects before them, when Mr. Ralph Nickleby suggested, that if they lost time, some more fortunate candidate might deprive Nicholas of the stepping-stone to fortune which the advertisement pointed out, and so undermine all their air-built castles. This timely reminder effectually stopped the conversation, and Nicholas having carefully copied the address of Mr. Squeers, the uncle and nephew issued forth together in quest of that accomplished gentleman; Nicholas firmly persuading himself that he had done his relative great

Unknown – "Advice from Rome" (*The Historical and Political Mercury)* (1702)

Hang up that sniveling, whining, maudlin Philosoper, *Heraclitus*: *Democritus* was in the Right; for **the World is a wide Stage, where nothing but Tragi-Comedy is acted**, and the generality of Mens Actions is rather to be laugh'd at than lamented. 'Tis a pleasant Dialogue in *Lucian*, where *Mercury* and *Charon*, after they had pil'd the Mountain *Ætna* upon *Pelion*, and *Parnassus* upon both, resolv'd from thence to take a View of all the World below. And first of all *Mercury* shews him the old *Cinque* and *Quarter*, *Milo* the *Crotonlate*, so highly applauded by the Greeks, for only carrying a Bull upon his Back: Then *Cyrus*, struggling for the Universal Monarchy of all *Asia*; then *Crœsus*, wallowing in Gold; and this, says he, is that precious Metal, for which Men Quarrel, Fight, and Murder one another. After this, he shews him the infinite Shoals and Multitudes of People as busie as Emmets upon a Molehill, having about them their chief Associates, Hope, Fear, and Madness; and all acting by the various Dictates of Pleasure, Avarice, Anger, Hatred, *&c.* which appear'd so Ridiculous to *Charon*, that he cry'd out, O *qualia Infœlicium Hominum Studia*! But what would the poor Ferriman have said, had *Mercury* shew'd him the Important Trifles, the Serious Baubles that employ the Wit, the Prudence, and Politicks of the Court of *Rome*. What a Coil is here begun afresh about the *Investiture*; *Fourbin* and *Veeda* have been again baiting the Holy Father to bestow it upon the Young Viceroy of *Spain*, *Philip* V. before he takes Shipping at *Barcelona* for *Naples*, as if it corruption into the heart, stagnates the noblest principles of action, irrecoverably, debases the sense of moral and religious obligation, and prevents us from living up to the height of our nature, because it prevents us from knowing its possible elevation. It cuts off all communication with virtue, and almost prevents the possibility of a return to it. If we do not rise as high as we aim, we shall rise the higher for having aimed at a lofty mark: but where the RULE is low, the practice cannot be high, though the converse of the proposition is not proportionably true.

Nothing more benumbs the exertions of ardent youthful virtue than the cruel sneer which worldly' prudence bestows on active goodness, and the cool derision it expresses at the defeat of a benevolent scheme, of which malice, -rather than penetration, had foreseen the failure. Alas! there is little need of any such discouragements. The world is a climate which too naturally chills a glowing generosity, and contracts an expanded heart. The zeal of the most sanguine is but too apt to cool, and the activity of the most diligent, to slacken of itself ;. and the disappointments which Benevolence encounters in the failure of her best-concerted projects, and the frequent depravity of the most chosen objects of her bounty, would soon dry up the amplest streams of charity, were they not fed by the living fountain of religious principle.

I cannot dismiss this part of my subject without animadverting on the too prompt alacrity, even of worthy people, to disseminate, in public and general conversation, instances of their unsuccessful brought out streaks, veins, and beauties in their characters not observable upon a cursory glance, while the reverse was the case with others. It thus happened, that without feeling any diminution in my general sentiment of goodwill towards mankind, my esteem for individuals frequently underwent a change.

In consequence of early noticing this, I contracted a great dislike to those half-wise rules and maxims which the aspirants for dominion over their fellow-creatures adopt as principles. Nothing, even now, so moves my spleen as to hear one class of men say that mankind should be ruled by their vices—that another can only be governed by their virtues—and that a true man of the world thinks he can only be safe in treating all men as rogues until they have proved their honesty: for experience has taught me that **the world is a collection of individuals, each of whom requires a different modification of jurisdiction**; a general law, therefore, must ever fall short, and be found defective, when that which is applicable to the species is applied to individuals.

But all this is a philosophy of riper years than belongs to the period of which I am treating. My first enterprise, after my determination to act more independently than I had previously conceived to be consistent with my duty, was a visit to Mr. Radamanthus Snarling. He had kindly, in the course of our walk from Mr. Latta's, invited me to come and see him, which I the more readily did, as what I had seen of him was undoubtedly to his advantage. His manners, as I have already mentioned, were exceemakes my very soul to burn within me,—and, coward and civilian though I be,—yes, a most intense and insuperable coward, prizing life and limb beyond all other earthly possessions, and loath to shed one single drop of blood either for my King or country,—yet such is the trumpet-power of the song of that son of genius, that I start from my old elbow-chair, up with the poker, tongs, or shovel, no matter which, and flourishing it round my head, cry,

"Charge, Chester, charge! On, Stanley, on!"

and then, dropping my voice, and returning to my padded bottom, whisper,

"Were the last words of Marmion!"

NORTH.

Bravo—bravo—bravo!

TICKLER.

I care not one single curse for all the criticism that ever was canted, or de canted, or recanted. Neither does the world. The world takes a poet as it finds him, and seats him accordingly above or below the salt. The world is as obstinate as a million of mules, and will not turn its head on one side or another for all the shouting of the critical population that ever was shouted. It is very possible that the world is a bad judge. Well then—appeal to posterity, and be hanged to you—and posterity will affirm the judgment, with costs.

NORTH.

How you can jabber away so, in such a temperature as this,

enough."

"Well, you've no business to," he said. "What do I want with a white-haired mother?"

"I'm afraid you'll have to put up with one, my lad," she said rather strangely.

They set off in great style, she carrying the umbrella William had given her, because of the sun. Paul, was considerably taller than she, though he was not big. He fancied himself.

On the fallow land the young wheat shone silkily. Minton pit waved its plumes of white steam, coughed, and rattled hoarsely.

"Now look at that!" said Mrs. Morel. Mother and son stood on the road to watch. Along the ridge of the great pit-hill crawled a little group in silhouette against the sky, a horse, a small truck, and a man. They climbed the incline against the heavens. At. the end the man tipped the waggon. There was an undue rattle as the waste fell down the sheer slope of the enormous bank.

"You sit a minute, mother," he said, and she took a seat on a bank, whilst he sketched rapidly. She was silent whilst he worked, looking round at the afternoon, the red cottages shining among their greenness.

"The world is a wonderful place," she said, "and wonderfully beautiful."

"And so's the pit," he said. "Look how it heaps together, like something alive almost—a big creature that you don't know."

"Yes," she said. "Perhaps!"

Speculations infinitely agreeable. I can sit behind this Counter, and fancy my little Shop, and the Transactions of it, an agreeable Representation of the grand Theatre of the World. When I see a Fool come in here, and throw away Fifty or an Hundred Guineas for a Trifle that is not really worth a Shilling, I am surpriz'd. But when I look out into the World, and see Lordships and Manors barter'd away for gilt Coaches and Equipage; an Estate for a Title; and an easy Freedom in Retirement for a servile Attendance in a Crowd; when I see Health with Eagerness exchanged for Diseases, and Happiness for a Game at Hazard; my Wonder ceases. Surely the World is a great Toy-shop, and all its Inhabitants run mad for Rattles. Nay, even the very wisest of us, however we may flatter ourselves, have some Failing or Weakness, some Toy or Trifle, that we are ridiculously fond of. Yet, so very partial are we to our own dear selves, that we overlook those Miscarriages in our own Conduct, which we loudly exclaim against in that of others; and, tho' the same Fool's Turbant fits us all,

You say that I, I say that you are He,

And each Man swears, "The Cap's not made for Me."

Gent. Ha! ha! 'Tis very true, indeed. But I imagine you now begin to think it Time to shut up Shop. Ladies, do you want any Thing else?

I La. No, I think not.—If you please to put up that Looking-glass, and the Perspective, I will pay you for them.

Gent. Well, Madam, how do you like this whimsical Humourist employment but thinking of you, as soon as I have quitted Madame de Sévigné; while we were together, we did nothing but talk of you incessantly, so that I am sure your ears must have tingled: you are the proper person to say which ear it was, for we mentioned you in every way in which it is possible to speak of a friend. I could not help accompanying her to the end of her first day's journey after leaving this place. I think we shall part with regret. But we shall soon see each other again; and if you do not come, we will pay you a visit together. In the mean time think of nothing that is likely to make you uneasy; seek after every thing that may give you pleasure, and do not be misled by the idea that there is nothing in life calculated to effect this: **the world is a very pretty thing, and he that seeketh findeth**. This is an assertion you may not credit: but I know what I know, and speak with more truth than you may imagine.

From Madame de Sévigné

This is a wise man; I tell him sometimes, seeing him as brisk as a bee, "My poor count, it is too early to go to bed yet; you are still very green, my honest friend. There is a strong dash of the old man, I mean of the young man, in you." But I must tell you the whole affair. The other day he made a very slight dinner, for he wanted to do penance, it seems, and in truth he has much need of it: by mere chance I happened to call him M. de Grignan; a name always, you know, at the tip of my tongue. He exclaimed, with great earnestness

William Mathews – *Getting on in the World, Or, Hints on Success in Life* (1874) i.

rustic who waited for the river to run by, they hesitate to embark in any business, or embark without spirit or hope. Had they lived a little earlier or a little later in the world's history, they could have "got on" without difficulty, but not at this epoch. They could have won fame or a fortune half a century ago, could win it, perhaps, half a century later, but not at this unlucky time. Success, always a coy maiden, is now, when crowds of wooers have made her saucy, harder than ever to win. The would-be poet, it is said, is always laboring under this disorder. He always somehow falls on evil days. The good time is either past or to come; it is never now. The truth is, however, that there is no occasion for these croakings, nor ever was at any period of the world's history. **The world is a hard world, but in the long run it is an eminently just one.** It is always groping about for men of ability and integrity to fill its places of responsibility, and those who have these qualifications, if they do not hide them from shyness, are almost sure to find employment. It always has been, and always will be, more difficult to find talents for the places than places for the talents. Human selfishness, were there no other agencies at work, will not suffer men of ability to languish in idleness.

Do not despair, then, because to win the prizes of life you must struggle against many competitors. Dryden says that no man ever need fear refusal from any lady, if he only give his heart to getting her ; and the same is true of success. As Lady Mary Wortley Montagu used to say, "If you wish to get on, you must do as you

William Mathews – *Getting on in the World, Or, Hints on Success in Life* (1874) ii.

and his life may be summed up in the words of Charles Lamb, who writes to a friend: "Coleridge is dead, and is said to have left behind him above forty thousand treatises on metaphysics and divinity,—not one of them complete!"

There is probably no more frequent cause of failure in life than that greediness which leads men to grasp at too many of its prizes. There are some the acquisition of which is incompatible with the acquisition of others, and the sooner this truth is realized and acted upon the better the chance of success and happiness. Much material good must be resigned if we would attain to the highest degree of moral excellence, and many spiritual joys must be foregone if we resolve at all risks to win great material advantages. To strive for a high professional position, and yet expect to have all the delights of leisure; to labor for vast riches, and yet to ask for freedom from anxiety and care, and all the happiness which flows from a contented mind; to indulge in sensual gratification, and yet demand health, strength, and vigor; to live for self, and yet to look for the joys that spring from a virtuous and self-denying life,—is to ask for impossibilities. **The world is a market, where everything is marked at a settled price;** and whatever we buy with our time, labor, or ingenuity,—whether riches, ease, tranquillity, fame, integrity, or knowledge,—we must stand by our decision, and not, like children, when we have purchased one thing repine that we do not possess another which we did not buy. The unreasonableness of many persons in this matter is well illustrated by a passage in one

William De Britaine – *Human Prudence; Or, The Art by which a Man May Raise Himself and His Fortune to Grandeur* (1726) i.

Person so contemptible but it may be in his power to be your best Friend or your worst Enemy: No Enemy is contemptible enough to be despised, since the most despicable command greater Strength, Wisdom and Interest than their own, to assist in the Designs of Malice or Mischief. The Eagle is not safe in the Arms of *Jupiter*, the Day she offends the little *Beetle*. Have a care of an Ox before you, of an Ass behind you, and of the Priest on either side of you. If you do Courtesies to a Hundred Men, and disoblige but one, that one shall be more active to your ruin, than all the other shall be to serve you. Therefore if you will gain respect, turn Usurer, and make all Men enter into Obligations to you. The World is a Shop of Tools, of which the Wise Man only is the Master.

SECT. X. *Of* PASSION.

A Wise Man is a great Monarch, he hath an Empire within himself; Reason commands in chief, and possesses the Throne and Sceptre. All his Passions like Obedient Subjects do obey; tho' the Territories seem small and narrow; yet the Command and Royalty is great, and reaches farther than he that wears the Moon for his Crest, or the other that wears the Sun for his Helmet.

Latius regnes avidum abmando Spiritum, quam

Si Lybiam remotis Gadibus jungas,

Es uterque Pœnus seriat uni.

William De Britaine – *Human Prudence; Or, The Art by which a Man May Raise Himself and His Fortune to Grandeur* (1726) ii.

after? It's but a short-liv'd *Ephemera*; it's like a Rose, which in the Evening makes its Tomb of the Scarlet, of which in the Morning it made its Cradle: And where is that Dignity which the next Moment may not be laid in the Dust?

The Fortune of the greatest Men run not upon the *Helix* that still enlargeth, but on a Circle, when arriving to their Meridian, they decline in Obscurity, and fall under the Horizon again.

The World is a Comedy, the best Actors are those that represent their Parts most naturally; but the Wisest do not always act Kings and Great Lords, and are seldom the Heroes of the Play.

Advancements and Honours are not given according to Merit, but by Pleasure, and fortuitously: *Philip Comines* tells us, that at the Battel of *Mont'bery*, fought between *Lewis* the XI of *France*, and *Charles* Duke of *Burgundy*, some lost their Offices for flying, which were bestowed upon others that fled Ten Leagues beyond them. *Luynes* from a Gentleman in *Decimo Sexto*, was made a Duke, a Peer, and High Constable of *France*.

Euripides, when his Father told him he was Knighted, made his Reply, *Good Father, you have that which every Man may have for his Money*.

How many Players have I seen upon a Stage fit to be Noblemen, and how many Noblemen fit only to represent them? Why, this can Fortune do, she makes some Companions of her Chariot, who for desert should be Lackeys to her Ladyship.

William De Britaine – *Human Prudence; Or, The Art by which a Man May Raise Himself and His Fortune to Grandeur* (1726) iii.

will not seem new unto you; if you reflect on the Infelicities which happen to others, your own will seem but light to you.

If thou art disquieted at any thing, consider with thy self, is the thing of that worth, that for it I should so disturb my self, and lose my Peace and Tranquility?

Have you lost your Dignities? You have not lost them, but surrender'd them; they are the Favours of Fortune, rarely the Characters of Merit; they have no Goodness in them, but what he stamps on them that doth enjoy them: If he be not Good; they are not Dignities, but Indignities: It cannot be said that a Man lost his Dignities, but that they lost him that gave them that Denomination, and made them Dignities.

Consider things really as they are, and you can never be troubled for any of them: If you have a Glass, esteem it as a Glass, and that it may be broken, and then you will never be angry when it is broken.

As there is no Gain upon Earth, without some Loss; so there is no Loss without some Gain; if thou hast lost thy Wealth, thou hast lost some Trouble with it: Art thou degraded from thy Honour? Thou art likewise free from the stroke of Envy; set the Allowance against the Loss, and you shall find no great Loss.

The World is a Sea, where some Men are wrecked; but all are tossed with Winds, and subject to the agitation of the Waves; let it be your Prudence to gain such a safe Port, which may secure you which they possess; these titles are sacred and inviolable; not to acknowledge them would be to introduce confusion and destruction. The right of conquest, when it is not legalized by defence, is an unjust right, because it is the right of force; but the conquest effected, the crime remains attached to the usurper and to the conqueror; and his successors are not accountable for it. An invaded territory on which a nation has lived for ages, is become their inheritance. To deny this principle would be to plunge the world in a state of continual warfare. **The world is a permanent revolution**; every thing has changed by turns; one people have succeeded another; here one nation has been expelled—there it has been destroyed by the sword; here it has fallen under the yoke of a conqueror—there it has yielded to a foreign domination; from this spot, from the fall and wreck of a great people, have issued several nations which have been the lords of an immense territory; time brings the consent of generations, and the prescription of ages consecrates the alteration. To destroy or derange this order would be to produce alarming effects; each people, with arms in their hands, would reclaim the inheritance of their ancestors, and there would be no reason that would prevent the descendants of the people of the south, who, in the fifth century, were either expelled, or conquered, or plundered of the greater part of their territory by the people of Germany, from demanding the restoration of those rights and territories which had been wrested from their ancestors.

up treasures on earth, seeing that, even that, which takes both time and pains of gathering, a few moments will undo and waste to nothing; then, where is their labour? I think a man or woman, in their gathering the world, is like a spider working its web; O what pains doth it take in spinning it out! and when it is spun, it sits down in the midst of it to take its rest; but when the maid comes to sweep the room, one touch of the besom sweeps it clean away, as if it had not been.

O but the world be a foolish thing to trust to! and they are the greatest of fools that trust to it: they are fools in these three respects. 1st, it is known to the world that the world is a very uncertain friend to listen to; for though it be a fair promiser, yet it is an ill performer, it is both a cheat and a liar. What though it promise pleasure and satisfaction to the owners thereof! It is but a mere cheat, for we see that none have more sorrow, than those who have it; what trouble and vexation have they in gathering of it? What weary care and anxiety in keeping of it? Though sometimes, let them keep all their hands about it, yet it will away. Riches take unto themselves wings, and oftentimes take the flight when there is most need of them, and that is when old age and sickness comes on: that motto cannot be written upon the world, "A friend in the time of need." I remember a very good observation one hath on the world; speaking to those that made a god of it, he said, it was a token of great wisdom to keep the god they chused; but it is a sign of the greatest folly, to chuse a god they cannot keep. 2dly, They are thing he hesitates to disclose, He has erred! his heart speaks, it is high-handed crime! He looks upon her affectionately, a forced smile spreads itself over his face. How forcibly it tells its tale. "Speak out," she continues, tremulously: "I am a sister; a sister cannot betray a brother's secrets." She removes her hand and lays it gently upon his shoulder.

Looking imploringly in her face for a few minutes, he replies as if it were an effort of great magnitude." Something you must not know—nor must the world! Many things are buried in the secrets of time that would make great commotion if the world knew them. It were well they passed unknown, for **the world is like a great stream with a surface of busy life moving on its way above a troubled current, lashing and foaming beneath, but only breaking hero and there as if to mark the smothered conflict.** And yet with me it is nothing, a moment of disappointment creeping into my contemplations, transplanting them with melancholy—"

"Something more!" interrupted Franeonia, "something more; it is a step beyond melancholy, more than disappointment. Uncle feels it sensibly—it pains him, it wears upon him. I have seen it foremost in his thoughts." Her anxiety increases, her soft meaning eyes look upon him imploringly, she fondles him with a sister's tenderness, the tears trickling down her cheeks as she beholds him downcast and in sorrow. His reluctance to disclose the secret becomes more painful to her.

"You may know it soon enough," he replies. "I have erred, and others that pure and lovely nature I found in you alone; and, when I shall lament the pride, the prejudice, the principles, that now forbid my rendering your situation as estimable in the eyes of the world as you are dear to my senses and my soul! But it must not be, sweet Ida! **the world is a terrific umpire**; I have made it the judge of my actions, and furnished it hitherto by my precepts, by my axioms, and example, with arms that would now turn against myself. Ida! my wife thou canst never be; but if thy national character is—" He abruptly stopt his half articulated soliloquy; he perceived a white and shadowy form moving among the trees: emerging from their shade, it glided towards the portico. From the pliant graces of its movement it could be no other than Ida: her left arm supported the elbow of her right, on which her cheek reposed; she walked slowly; languishment and gentle weariness hung upon her motions, and touched her figure with a pensive softness. She paused as she approached the bath room, and gazed on the delicious scenes around her, on which the sweet repose of nature seemed to hang. She turned her eyes towards the bath, and seemed tempted by the luxury it presented; she threw aside her veil to breathe a freer air. She approached the bath, and raising the scarlet drapery of its curtain, held it for some time with a doubtful and hesitating air; then, unbinding the roses that drooped on her brow, she approached the couch, and beheld it already occupied. Her first impulse from surprise, from confusion, was to fly; her next was regulated by the simplicity and innocent confidence that always the rest of mankind. He should see that those less fortunate must ultimately turn to him for guidance and light.

Education, simply put, is but the equipment of man with the foundations of truth. And yet, too, it means a training that provides the necessary data in the light of which he shall choose just what commodity he shall supply to that market-exchange we call humanity.

What is Success?

For education is the acquisition of light, and light means growth, development, life. And life is but the science of relationships. **The world is a vast market-place where human needs and desires create demands that must be supplied.** And what is success but the ability to meet the demands that civilization makes upon humanity? Opportunity is nothing but the disunited elements of a distinct need, and an ability to fill that need. Success means yet more, for it contemplates the union of those elements and shows itself synonymous with service.

This means that we must "know ourselves" even as the motto of the philosophical Greeks demanded it. This involves the element of ability or power, and is subjective. Yet we must understand our relationship to society and her needs, which is objective. Here we have, at the risk of being needlessly analytical, the great potential energy which is often unhappily defined as education, and a channel through which our energies might flow, which is defined as opportunity for service. But in no sphere has for why should men steal who are free to make? It shall be set in a place of greenery, for **the world is a large place and its loveliness mostly a wilderness;** it shall be far enough away from its next for privacy and not too far for neighborliness; it shall have a little space knit within a garden wall; flowers shall creep up to its warmth, and flow, guided, but unrebuked, over wall and low-drooped eaves. It shall neither be built in poverty and haste, nor abandoned in prosperity; it shall grow as the family grows; it shall have rooms enough for the privacy of each and the fellowship of all. Its arms shall spread wide enough to gather in a little measure of the common earth, for your democracy will provide leisure and your democrat will not only pluck flowers but will grow them, not only eat the fruits of the earth but will find joy in planting, in "seed time and harvest," and all the myriad days of growth between will look to the sundial rather than the timetable for the ordering of his day.

The rooms of his house shall be ample, and low, wide-windowed, deep-seated, spacious, cool by reason of shadows in summer, warm by the ruddy glow of firesides in winter, open to wistful summer airs, tight closed against the wintry blasts: a house, a home, a shrine; a little democracy unjealous of the greater world, and pouring forth the spirit of its own sure justness for the commonwealth.

Its walls shall be the quiet background for the loveliness of life, hung over with the few records of our own and others' growth made in the playtime of art; its furnishings the product of that art's

Look at the worldly and all who set themselves up above the people of God, has not God's image and His truth been distorted in them? They have science; but in science there is nothing but what is the object of sense. The spiritual world, the higher part of man's being is rejected altogether, dismissed with a sort of triumpth, even with hatred. The world has proclaimed the reign of freedom, especially of late, but what do we see in this freedom of theirs? Nothing but slavery and self-destruction! For the world says:

"You have desires and so satisfy them, for you have the same rights as the most rich and powerful. Don't be afraid of satisfying them and even multiply your desires." That is the modern doctrine of the world. In that they see freedom. And what follows from this right of multiplication of desires? In the rich, isolation and spiritual suicide; in the poor, envy and murder; for they have been given rights, but they have not been shown the means of satisfying their wants. They maintain that **the world is getting more and more united, more and more bound together in brotherly community, as it overcomes distance and sets thoughts flying through the air.**

Alas, put no faith in such a bond of union. Interpreting freedom as the multiplication and rapid satisfaction of desires, men distort their own nature, for many senseless and foolish desires and habits and ridiculous fancies are fostered in them. They live only for mutual envy, for luxury and ostentation. To have dinner, visits, carriages, rank and slaves to wait on one is looked upon as a

John Ryland – *The Preceptor, or Counsellor of Human Life: For the Use of the British Youth* (1776)

All its beauty and glory depends alone on fancy—all the world is a lye and a traitor—it betrays our hopes into vexation, and betrays our fouls into guilt and misery.

The world is a vexatious vanity.—There is vexation in getting riches, vexation in enjoying riches and pleasures, and vexation in losing them; and whether you get, or lose, you are always disappointed.

The vanity of the world appears, in that a little cross will imbitter great worldly comforts, and a moment's vexation will destroy all worldly joy. The vanity of the world appears, that the longer we enjoy worldly things, the more flat, insipid, and silly those things appear, and the more nauseous they grow.—The enjoyment of worldly pleasures is nothing else but a tedious repetition of the same thing, the same surfeits and shallow sensations—all the things of the world can stand us in no stead, at the sad times when we stand in most need of comfort, viz. they are vain and useless under terrors of conscience, and they are vain and useless at the hour of death.

The world is vain, as it is unsuitable to the soul of man. The soul is a spirit, the world is dead dross—the soul is immortal, the world is perishing—beauty, health, and pleasure all perish. The necessities of the soul are all of a quite different kind than what this world can supply. The world is full of inconstancy and fickleness; there is no stability in any thing, no certainty in any worldly comforts.

Anonymous – "Song 86" (*The British Songster*) (1782)

How pleasant a sailor's life passes,
    Who roams o'er the water main!
No treasure he ever amasses,
    But cheerfully spends all his gain.
We're strangers to party and faction,
    To honour and honesty true,
And would not commit a base action,
    For power or profit in view.
        Then why should we quarrel for riches,
            Or any such glittering toys?
        A light heart and a thin pair of breeches
            Goes through the world, brave boys.

The world is a beautiful garden,
    Enrich'd with the blessings of life,
The toiler with plenty rewarding;
    Which plenty too often breeds strife.
When terrible tempests assail us,
    And mountainous billows affright,
No grandeur or wealth can avail us,
    But skilful industry steers right.
                Then why should, &c.

The courtier's more subject to dangers,
    Who rules at the helm of the state,
Than we, that, to politics strangers,
    Escape the snares laid for the great.
The various blessings of nature,
    In various nations we try,
No mortals than us can be greater,
    Who merrily live till we die.
                Then why should, &c.

their paradoxical, mystical, and metaphysical theories. One morning I saw my friend sitting under the acacias on the terrace in front of the house in which Gibbon had lived, and where he wrote the 'Decline and Fall.' He said, "I am trying to sharpen my wits in this pungent air which gave such a keen edge to the great historian, so that I may fathom this book. Your modern poets, Byron, Scott, and Moore, I can read and understand as I walk along, but I have got hold of a book by one now that makes me stop to take breath and think." It was Shelley's 'Queen Mab.' As I had never heard that name or title, I asked how he got the volume. "With a lot of new books in English, which I took in exchange for old French ones. Not knowing the names of the authors, I might not have looked into them, had not a pampered, prying priest smelt this one in my lumber-room, and, after a brief glance at the notes, exploded in wrath, shouting out 'Infidel, jacobin leveller: nothing can stop this spread of blasphemy but the stake and the fagot; the world is retrograding into accursed heathenism and universal anarchy!' When the priest had departed, I took up the small book he had thrown down, saying, 'Surely there must be something here worth tasting.' You know the proverb 'No person throws a stone at a tree that does not bear fruit.'"

"Priests do not," I answered; "so I, too, must have a bite of the forbidden fruit. What do you think of it?"

"To my taste," said the bookseller, "the fruit is crude, but well flavoured; it requires a strong stomach to digest it; the writer is an for it. I am catching mullets of a pound weight, friend. You'd be delighted, if you were here, to see them. Get into that bucket, and look.' The wolf thereupon jumped into the other bucket, and, being the heavier of the two, immediately sunk to the bottom. He, in his way *down*, seeing his boon companion rising up with equal rapidity, cried 'Halloo, my friend, where are you going? are we not fish together in this well?' 'My friend,' replied the fox, 'the world is a pair of scales, and every body in it is sometimes high and sometimes low.' So the poor wolf was left behind, and the fox got off: but soon afterwards he was caught by a farmer, and then made a merit of the exploit, and demanded a reward for having destroyed the wolf. 'Not so, my friend,' said the farmer, 'though your treason has succeeded, the traitor is not a bit the more agreeable:' and he immediately hung up the cunning rascal by the neck."

It is much to be wished that Lionfante had followed, in all things, the farmer's example. However, he contents himself with confining Gano; and afterwards, on consulting his prisoner Astolpho what he should do with him, sends him off to Charles with a guard, and an account of his treason. On the road, he unfortunately found leisure to frame another story, by which the *wise* Emperor was deceived; Astolpho's guilt more firmly believed than ever; and no credit at all given to the admiral's honesty.

Meanwhile, the army of Meridiana and the Paladins arrived at Paris, and soon another face of things was seen. How they were received by Charles; how they rescued their brother warriors who be found in it. It is far from being my wish to damp that lively glow of feeling, which at so early a period of your life you naturally cherish. I am only anxious wisely to regulate it, and to prevent its excess from, occasioning to you severe mortification on discovering that neither persons nor things, as you will meet with them in the world, are exactly such as you now flatter yourselves that you shall find them to be. It is not my wish to give you an unfavourable opinion of the state of society and of mankind in general. But it is necessary for you to know, that **the world is a mixed state of good and evil**, and that the beings who inhabit it, and with whom you must associate, partake of the same heterogeneous qualities. The vision of futurity, which your ardent imaginations paint to you in such gay colours, appears, no doubt, to be indescribably fascinating. Not a cloud can be seen in your glowing horizon. No shade over casts the enchanting landscape, in the midst of which you are placed. And it has probably never occurred to you that you may possibly meet with some thorns in the flowery path which you are now treading. A few years will in all likelihood prove to you the extreme fallacy of such sentiments.—But I flatter myself that you will obtain this knowledge, rather from the valuable maxims of reflection and wisdom which you have treasured up in our minds, than from the rough discipline of the world. I hope it will not be necessary for you to plunge into all the excesses of fashionable amusements, generally denominated pleasures, to be convinced that, so far from deriving substantial happiness from them, they have more

Benjamin Steel, "Poetry of Ebeneezer Elliott" (1834)

All poets are poets of the poor. For, is not the whole human race a poor race, subject to sin, sorrow, and death? Princes are paupers, autocrats, almsmen—and they know they are, in spite of their subjects or slaves. **The world is a workhouse, and its rulers overseers**. Their high mightinesses, the magistrates, are all accountable to the cholic; and, even in this life, obedient to the diet of worms. Who but a fool dare lift up his voice and say, "I am rich," when palsy at the very moment may wring is mouth awry, or apoplexy smite him into a breathing clod Strip the rich man of his purple and fine linen—and what an exposure of shrivelled skin—marrowless bones—flesh not like grass, but straw! Beauty, thought, intellect, genius, virtue—what, in this mysterious life of ours—what even are they? Shut your eyes and open them, and what a ghastly transfiguration! In their room, loathsomeness, imbecility, idiocy, insanity, vice, wretchedness, and woe; and is it not enough of itself to convince us in our worst pride, that we are all most miserably poor, to think that the round earth is not merely trenched all over with our graves, but composed of our very dust?

This is one light in which humanity may be truly viewed, if there be truth in the Two Testaments. And in no other light could it be truly viewed, if we do not believe in a Future State. Now, the ancient—the heathen world, did not believe in a Future State—though it did all it could—strove with all its mind, heart, and soul, so to believe—deified heroes—and changed them into stars. Imagination created its own mythologies, fluctuating between heathe tears he sheds over his tyrannous destiny."

Agrippa was a deep observer and admirer of external nature, and of all her phenomena, and had often gazed upon the scene which the stranger described, but the feelings and ideas which it awakened in the mind of the latter were so different from anything that he had himself experienced, that he could not help, for a reason, gazing upon him in speechless wonder. His guest, however, speedily resumed the discourse,

"But I trouble you; then to the purpose of making my visit. I have heard strange tales of a wondrous mirror, which your potent art has enabled you to construct, in which, whomsoever looks may see the distant or the dead, on whom he desires again to fix his gaze. My eyes see nothing in this outward visible world which can be pleasing to their sight ; the grave has closed over every thing that once contributed to my enjoyment. The world is a vale of tears, but among all the tears which water that sad valley, not one is shed for me; the fountain in my own heart, too, is dried up. I would once again look; upon the face which I loved. I would see that eye more bright, and that step more stately than the antelope; that brow, the broad smooth page on which God had inscribed its fairest characters. I would gaze on all I loved and all I lost. Such a gaze would be dearer to my heart than all the world has to offer me, except the grave! —except the grave!!

The passionate pleading of the stranger had such an effect upon Agrippa, who was not used to exhibit his miracles of art to the extreme want. Domestic affections depend on association. We love an object if, as often as we see or recollect it, an agreeable sensation arises in our minds. But alas! how should he glow with the charities of father and husband, who gaining scarcely more than his own necessities demand, must have been accustomed to regard his wife and children, not as the soothers of finished labour, but as rivals for the insufficient meal? In a man so circumstanced the tyranny of the present can be over powered only by the tenfold mightiness of the future. Religion will cheer his gloom with her promises, and by habituating his mind to anticipate an infinitely great revolution hereafter, may prepare it even for the sudden reception of a less degree of melioration in this world.

But if we hope to instruct others, we should familiarize our own minds to some fixed and determinate principles of action. **The world is a vast labyrinth, in which almost every one is running a different way, and almost every one manifesting hatred to those who do not run the same way.** A few indeed stand motionless, and not seeking to lead themselves or others out of the maze, laugh at the failures of their brethren. Yet with little reason: for more grossly than the most bewildered wanderer does he err, who never aims to go right. It is more honourable to the head, as well as to the heart, to be misled by our eagerness in the pursuit of truth, than to be safe from blundering by contempt of it. The happiness of man kind is the end of virtue, and truth is the knowledge of the means; which he will never seriously attempt to discover, who has not habitually us, or that the spirit of an affectionate parent hovers over us—that one or more of our friends frequently look into our chambers, or our closets, and observe our actions? Is such liberty contrary to the laws of the invisible world? If it is not, and our secret actions are laid open to the world of spirits, as well as to the broad eye of Him who will bring every idle word into judgment, "what manner of persons ought we to be in all holy conversation and godliness."

How awful then is our situation! and how necessary it is to withdraw to inspect our actions, and seek for grace, to live unblameably in it. For "**the world**," says an English writer, "**is a troubled ocean**; and who can erect stable purposes on its fluctuating waves?" **The world is a school of wrong**; and who does not feel himself warping to its pernicious influences? On this sea of glass, how insensibly we slide from our own steadfastness! Some sacred *truth*, which was struck in lively characters on our souls, is obscured if not obliterated. Some worthy *resolution*, which heaven had wrought in our hearts, is shaken if not overthrown. Some enticing *vanity*, which we had solemnly renounced, again practices its wiles and captivates our affections. How often has a word of applause dropt lucious poison into our ears; or some disrespectful expression raised a gust of passion in our bosoms? Our innocence is of so tender a constitution that it suffers in the promiscuous crowd. Our purity is of so delicate a complexion that it scarce touches on the world without contracting a slain. We see, we hear with peril.

But here *safety* dwells. Every meddling and intrusive avo-

Thomas Miller – "Song of the Outlaws" (1837)

Come, fill the brown bowl, boys, let care abide the morrow,
For life's but a shaft that flies feathered with sorrow,
And Love is a hart, that hides far from the glade,
So timid at first that he shuns his own shade: —
Our bodies are bows, and we laugh, drink, and sing.
Just to ease the bent wood, boys, and slacken the string;
Then, fill the brown bowl, boys, and let it go round,
Lest the bow-string should snap with too sudden a bound.
Oh! the world is a greenwood, in which we all dwell;
Some know all its wild-paths, some tread but the dell:
And they who have found its broad beaten highway,
Oft sigh for the shade in the heat of the day:
Ambition grows weary and pines for the glen,
Where he sported in childhood — 'mid happiness then —
And Fame throws behind him a lingering look —
As the hunted stag glances when passing the brook.
'Tis better to fall at the head of the herd,
Than fly back and perish, unmourned, uninterr'd;
'Tis better to die, grasping arrow and bow,
Amid those that we love, than be slave to a foe:
To be bound with the brave amid Victory's sheaves.
Than to wither the last ear the reaper's hand leaves:
For life is the target at which Death's shafts fly,
If they miss us, we live — if they hit us, we die.
If we die in the greenwood, the sound of the horn

little duodecimo, which, travelling far beyond the range limited to the more ponderous folio or quarto, finds its way into every nook, and village of the land,—she has given a portability and increased circulation to the merchandize of mind, and vindicated the claim of the aspiring student to a participation in the glories and emoluments of the actual world, superadding to those pleasures which descend upon him in the visions of his study, the more solid gratifications of this sublunary sphere.

It is all very well for the ignorant bustler — the man of margins and red tape,—to deride the acquirements, which he does not possess, and the taste, with which he is not imbued. It is easy for him to say that **the business of the world is a dry routine of details,** unsusceptible of the embellishments of Literature, or the polish of science—and, that the highly-gifted with intellect and erudition are little fitted to grapple with the tangible realities of life. He may probably, should his reading extend so far, cite the case of Addison, an inefficient Secretary of State,—or Cowper, a shame-faced Clerk of the House of Lords. But, to say nothing of the constitutional peculiarities which disabled those great and virtuous men for the avocations of public life, let him turn to Locke and Gibbon, Lords Commissioners of Trade,—to Clarendon, equally great and dignified, as Historian, Chancellor, and Prime Minister,—to Raleigh, over whose checquered and romantic career, his literary and scientific pursuits have shed a lustre, which no time can dim,—to Grotius, the benefactor of his country in the manifold and seemingtestable, impious, and tyrannical outrages, invasions, confiscations, rapines, and massacres, of the French Government, has not the partition of Poland been cited as a parallel! It has really, Sir, been called into service so often, that it ought no longer to be considered as a *pair*. It is time to agree, that at least in any future enormities of France, she shall not have a set-off in the partition of Poland.

But after all, to what does this argument a best amount? **The world is a bad world**, and we are, therefore, to withdraw ourselves from it. Good:—if this were, indeed, practicable; if it remained for use to choose whether we would make a part of this world or no;

"If Heav'n would make us such another world
"Of one entire and perfect chrysolite,"—

where all should be pure, and perfect, and without a flaw. But if we are, in spite of ourselves, compelled to belong to the world in which we are placed, I know not whether it be not more manly, more statesman-like, and more virtuous too, to make the best of it;—to do what we can with the materials which we have; and to endeavour to work out our own happiness,—even though we should not be able to separate and disconnect it from the happiness of our fellow creatures.

I think this a more rational conduct than the sort of *national secession* which the honourable gentleman's motion goes to recommend. I know of no justifiable reason for such a *secession*,—I can conceive no motive for it, consistent with true sense of right, and just dignity of character. I know not how we could reconcile it honours of learning; this is the mighty recompense by which mothers and governesses stimulate indolence and encourage talent. Marriage may, in a twofold sense, be called the *end* of all this toil; for it is not only its object, but its termination. The goal once reached, ambition becomes extinct. Acquirements gained by painful industry are relinquished as distasteful, or pursued as an occasional amusement. **The dissipations of the world abundantly occupy time**; and that vacancy of the mind and abundance of accomplishments coexist more frequently than is generally suspected, is a truth which the husband begins to find gradually dawning on his understanding when knowledge comes too late.

Catharine Vernon, though the inhabitant of a cottage, had not been a recluse. In the society of her mother she had visited France, Switzerland, and Italy, improving her knowledge, and enlarging her ideas. She possessed, in an eminent degree, that least cultivated of all accomplishments, the art of agreeable companionship. She conversed well, because she had within her the elements of conversation, ideas. People complain of the emptiness of "female talk;" they must search a little farther to arrive at the root of the matter, and then, peradventure, they may complain of the empty-ness of female heads; well would it be if complaint produced remedy.

If half the pains that are expended on teaching girls to play well, sing well, and dance well, were employed in teaching them to talk well, men would have companions instead of playthings, and one she esteemed and loved was escaping from the severity of a sorrow which Catharine now was well able to comprehend.

Rachel wrote thus:—

"If my former letters, dearest Catharine, have been occupied chiefly with your interests, and inquiries after all that amuses or surprises you, in a mode of existence of which my imagination,—always a sober painter,—cannot even conceive a picture;—if, as you complain, I have said little of Golding Magna or its inhabitants,—it has been because I was reluctant to touch on topics which I knew most excited your curiosity,—shall I not rather say your sympathy?—while so much uncertainty involved them. Now that feelings,—and feelings, in the High Street of Golding Magna, must, you are aware, constitute my events,—which have hitherto been fluctuating, seem to become more steady;—now that I can write what will contribute to your satisfaction, I fear I am in danger of wearying you with egotism. I have much to tell, and the temptation of opening to you thoughts which none around me would pardon, or perhaps understand, is too strong to be resisted. I know that you love me, and I do believe that you will rejoice to learn, that a prospect of happiness opens to me sufficient to satisfy the humble hopes of one who knows that, at least, **this world is a succession of trials.** To be the first, sole occupant of kit heart, might have filled me with overweening self-confidence. I might have learned to value too highly those poor endowments which had attracted him, and I am satisfied to believe that it was necessary to the security of my the circles ten years since. At seventeen she was beloved by Sir Greville, if not with the reality of first love, at least with all its devotedness. It would be too ridiculous to suppose that he, with his infinite advantages, had lived to be five-and-twenty without previous, and, perhaps, extensive experience of *la belle passion*. Nevertheless, Lady Sophia had the advantage of being his first *fiancée*, which is much the same."

"It is," acquiesced Catharine, with a sigh.

"But I do not expect in you, Catharine, the childish romance of believing, that because he loved Lady Sophia before even the fact of your existence was known, he therefore loved her more. All the sing-song nonsense of first-love, of which one used to read in trashy romances, has gone by with moonshine soliloquies and sonnets. **The world has outlived its babyhood**, and we look for common sense even from tolerably well-educated girls, whether in their teens or their twenties."

"You are angry," said Catharine, raising her eye with that expression of serene integrity so peculiar to her noble countenance, "because I appear less happy than usual—less satisfied or less at ease with Cleveland. But you mistake the cause. He was aware that I could not avoid over hearing Mr. Stark's letter read by the dutchess, or her comments on it, and I think he should have considered my feelings sufficiently to have spoken openly to me afterward. It is not of a former attachment that I complain; I am not young enough to indulge for a moment the dream of being the first with a mother's kindness, but she found no words of congratulation, for there was no hope of future happiness in her heart.

"Lady Sophia never loved him as I love him," said Catharine, with fervour; "did she not sacrifice his happiness to her pride?—entail years of misery for what, after all, was a fault,—a fault now, not only pardoned, but forgotten by herself? What possible error could alienate me from him?"

"If it were crime?" said Mrs. Warren, still in tears.

"Crime!—no; that is not within the compass of possibility!—That might indeed effect our separation, and leave for me the single refuge of the grave; but crime cannot taint the name of Cleveland!"

"The world pardons its prosperous children, and has courtly names for their lapses from rectitude, which are branded with strong stigmas when low men fall," said Mrs. Warren, sorrowfully. "Error may entail dreadful—awful consequences."

"But are not human actions to be judged by the principle,—not the effect?" said Catharine, with strong emotion. "Were we accountable for all the evil that resulted from our actions, even the best of them might be recorded against us as sins, and the fallibility of man would be a reproach to the justice of Providence."

"Effects which may in some degree be foreseen, become parts of actions," returned Mrs. Warren. "However, my dear child, to descend from generals to particulars, let me assure you that the error or fault, whichever we may term it, that dissolved the engagement of Sir Greville and Lady Sophia, was no inexpiable of-the ruin of the past—arrived at the lees of the cup of life—to him a rich draught, but quaffed all too quickly—mingled with the poison that exhilarates and destroys," said Lord Vere, with an air meant to be melancholy. "How I could moralize, if I dared inflict my tediousness on you!"

"Pray endeavour to be amusing," said the beautiful Augusta; "I have been wearied to death with these eternal Hamiltons the whole morning."

"One would really imagine you dreaded a rival near the throne, Augusta," said Lady Sophia.

"Forbid it, heaven!—the heaven of love and fashion!" said Lord Vere, with mock emphasis. "A rustic from the Highlands would bring her rural graces in vain among us, I fancy, but that the pebble is set in gold—and the world, in this age of political economy, has grown more than ever mercenary. *Apropos des bottes*—have you seen Lawton this morning?"

"Not this week," said Lady Sophia, "which may be explained by the fact that we saw him every day for the previous fortnight, and he would tire of the same faces even in Elysium."

"True; change is to him the vital principle, and he literally goes about, like the Athenians, inquiring for some new thing! Somebody has given him a glowing description of the new heiress, and as his imagination has sufficient food to occupy itself withal, he is almost in love through expectation. He would have been a worshipper of Mokanna, if the veiled prophet had been among the cheats of our their future mother," said Colonel Hamilton, with that severity of manner which, in him, always indicated deep feeling of the most painful nature. "In the first era of her life, the character of woman influences principally her own happiness, for even that of parents, for the most part, is affected by children *in the aggregate*, not by one child in particular. In her second era, its effects reach a more extended point—a point still—the happiness of that other human, moral, responsible agent, her husband. But in the third, the great era of woman's destiny—*her age* of empire—when the duties of maternity demand her exertions—then, indeed, her role becomes the most important which an accountable being can sustain; affecting, by the manner in which it is sustained, not only the mortal but the immortal interests of those on whose minds she makes the first impressions; the *rasœ tabulœ* on which she traces characters permanent often beyond the reach of time or circumstance. **The destinies of the world are more in the hands of woman than we in our masculine pride are always willing to admit.** *She* moulds the wax when it is most ductile; *she* prepares our successors, the future controllers of the earth. It is as a mother that woman must always appear to philosophers and politicians most interesting, most important."

"Reflection only can make us comprehend how awful a thing it is to hold the deposit of the happiness of a fellowcreature," said Catharine, pale from the strong emotion with which she had listened to her husband; "even the temporal happiness; and carry-you find that, and disposition is satisfied, there rest your purposes and perseverance, in spite of all discouragements; for there you will grow, and there only you will flourish, and no doubt, prepare a soil for those who may come after you, that they at least, may have a less fugitive fortune."

The tone of this discourse took Hector by surprise, he never before having heard the chief so philosophical. "Pray go on, sir," he said, "and give me fully your thoughts. I feel sensibly the want of a few aphorisms of experience, as a nucleus to my own crude meditations upon that world of which I as yet know so little."

"The world is a strange gathering, which I but little understand myself," continued the laird," and man an animal more difficult to describe than any other of the more uniform productions of nature. But this you will find, that though none of nature's productions require the exercise of sympathy, or the energies of mutual support, so much as man, none exercise the feeling so little, or so often turn it strangely against those to whom it would be most valuable."

"I suppose that is true sir," said Hector, as the chief paused: "but pray go on."

"To proceed with my allegory, then," Glenmore continued; "while the oak of the wood suffers itself to be twined about by many sapplings, which it seems proud to support, and which add grace to its trunk, the reverse of this holds true in the world; for the strong oak among men, who is himself rooted firm and can defy the blast, surrounds himself with a circle of exclusion, which poisons or cru-

Alphonse de Lamartine – *A Pilgrimage to the Holy Land* (1835)

To travel in search of wisdom, was a sort of proverb among the ancients; but it is not understood among us. They travelled not merely in search of unknown dogmas and lessons of philosophy, but to see and to judge everything. For my part I am constantly struck with the narrow and petty view we take of the institutions and customs of foreign nations; and if my mind has been enlarged —if my views have been extended—if I have learned to tolerate things by understanding them, I owe all these advantages to my frequent changes of scene and points of view. To study past ages in history, men by travelling, and God in nature—that is the grand school. We study everything in our miserable books, and com pare every thing with our petty local habits. And who have made our habits and our books? Men who knew as little as ourselves. Let us open the Book of books! Let us live, see, and travel! **The world is a book of which we turn a page at every step**. How little must he know who has turned but one page!

***

DAMASCUS

April 2nd, 1833.

Dressed in the Arabic costume, I this morning traversed the principal quarters of Damascus, ac companied only by M. Baudin, for we were fearful that the appearance of a numerous party of strangers would attract attention to us. We passed a considerable copyist. You grant then, that the hope is not visionary; the scheme is not impracticable. Our purpose is to realize this picture, and you concede that that purpose will be accomplished. And what auxiliary more effective, could the missionary enterprise desire, than Liberia presents? Here may be the grand depot of resources; the great organization of plans. What fitter place, for the herald of Christianity to rest his foot, and replume his wing for his flight into the dark interior?

But it is not in revelation alone, that I read noble promises of renovation for Africa. He studies men and things carelessly and coldly, who does not discover consoling lessons of hope for the future. The series of past history,—the progressive character of the human mind,—the successively brightening dispensations of Providence tell me, that **the world is a school whose bitterest lessons have been learned, and whose brightest are yet to come**. Does any man believe that Africa shall not yet show a brighter page, or fear that perpetual darkness is to wrap her fair fields and fertile vales? No; the genius of the age,—the spirit of Christian enterprise,—the character, the command, and the promises of Heaven forbid it, and cheer us on in the prosecution of our great design. It has been the fortune of Liberia to live down objection, and to stand in herself their triumphant refutation. An eminent and revered character, who has avowed a change of views, adverse to the Colonization Society, has stated that by the non-consent or unanimous opposition of the colored people of this country, "the society is

Lord Byron – "Epigram" (1821)

The world is a bundle of hay
    Mankind are the asses who pull;
Each tugs it a different way
        And the greatest of all is John Bull.

rather brought to a stand-still, by the conflicting testimony of Mr. and Mrs. Simkin, the next step was to consider what was to be done. It is very awkward that there is no such thing as keeping a secret. Fitzgeorge would have given anything, if he had had any thing to give, that this investigation should not be made public, but it was absolutely impossible to prevent it; for it had been talked about so much, that all the world knew that it was going on, and all the world was on the tiptoe of expectation for the important result. All the world is a queer creature; it seems to have nothing to do, but to interest itself about that which does not concern it. Two hundred years ago, the people who lived in this island burnt witches;—what will the people of this island laugh at two hundred years hence?

One section of the committee carried the report of the investigation to the Honourable Augustus Fitzgeorge, and the other carried it to Lord Fitzgeorge. When Augustus Fitzgeorge had read it over, he was most graciously pleased to be exceedingly indignant, and had not some of the party been his particular friends, he would have thrown the papers at their heads.

"This is an absolute nuisance," said he; the world is looking for a corroboration of certain reports that are in circulation, and this all but contradicts them."

"Not quite contradicts, however," replied one of the party. "Mr. Simkin contends for Thomson, and Mrs. Simkin will have it that Jackson was the favourite. Is it not possible that they were both faa social chat. SHANE FADH tells his own story, which commences in the following manner: —

"Well, Shane," said Andy Morrow, "will you give us an account of your wedding ? I'm tould it was the greatest *let- out* that ever was in the country, or since."

"And you may say that, Mr. Morrow," said Shane, "I was at many a wedding myself, but never at the likes of my own, barring Tim Lanigan's that married Father Corrigan's niece."

"When I was a *brine-oge*," [a young man full of fun and frolic] said Shane, "I was as wild as an unbroken cowlt—no devilment was too hard for me; and signs on it, for there was'nt a piece of mischief done in the parish, hut was laid at my door, and the dear knows I had my own to answer for, let alone to be set down for that of other people: but any way there was many a thing done in my name, when I knew neither act nor part about it. Mary was then as purty a girl as you'd meet in a fair—indeed I think I'm looking at her, with her fair flaxen ringlets hanging over her shoulders, as she used to pass our house, going to mass, of a Sunday. God rest her sowl she's now in glory. Many a happy day we passed together; and I could take it to my death, that an ill word, let alone to raise our hands to one another, never passed between us........."

The world is a strange thing—myself hardly knows what to make of it! It's I that did doat night and day upon that girl; and indeed there was them that could have seen me in Jimmaiky for her sake, for she was the beauty of the country, not to say of the parish,

Samuel F. Green – "Affection, the Season of Beauty" (1832)

I.

The flowers, the delicate daughters of earth,
From the genial spring date their beautiful birth;
Awaked by the zephyrs, and woo'd by the sun,
In the sweetest of seasons their reign is begun.

II.

Through the summer and autumn the zephyrs still rise,
And the sun, like a bridegroom, still glows in the skies,
And still shew the flowers as fragrant as fair,
The pride of the earth, the perfume of the air.

III.

But the rude winds of winter the zephyrs succeed,
And the cold and the gloom the sun's glory impede,
And the flowers unfriended to bare ruin haste:
The sky is inclement, the world is a waste.

IV.

So the charms of the tender and beautiful maid
By a season's vicissitude flourish and fade;
Affection's sweet birth, its bright beams they expect,
And die in the winter of cruel neglect.

ordinary than to observe with what obtuse, dull, and common-place impressions most men pass through this wonderful life, which Heaven has ordained for us. Life, which, to such a mind, means every thing momentous, mysterious, prophetic, monitory, trying to the reflections, and touching to the heart, to the many is but a round of cares and toils, of familiar pursuits and formal actions. Their fathers have lived; their children will live after them; the way is plain; the boundaries are definite; the business is obvious; and this to them is life. They look upon this world as a vast domicile, as an extensive pleasure- ground; the objects are familiar; the implements are worn; the very skies are old; the earth is a pathway for those, that come and go, on earthly errands; the world is a working field, a ware house, a market-place—and this is life!

But life indeed—the intellectual life, straggling with its earthly load, coming, it knows not whence, going it knows not whither, with an eternity unimaginable behind it, with an eternity to be experienced before it, with all its strange and mystic remembrances, now exploring its past years as if they were periods before the flood, and then gathering them within a space as brief and unsubstantial as if they were the dream of a day—with all its dark and its bright visions of mortal fear and hope; life, such a life, is full of mysteries. In the simplest actions, indeed, as well as in the loftiest contemplations in the most ordinary feelings, as well as in the most abstruse speculations, mysteries meet us every where, mingle with all our employments, terminate all our views.

Unknown – "Varieties" in *The Monthly Traveller* (1830)

COMPANY.—The difference between what is called ordinary company and good company, is only hearing the same tiling in a little room or a large saloon, at small tables or at great tables, before two candles or twenty sconces.

PUNNING.—A gentleman, says a late London paper, walking past Westminster bridge, inquired how the bridge answered. The reply was ready and witty—"if you'll step to the gate you'll be *toll'd.*"

SIMILARITY OF SENTIMENT.—There is nothing wanting to make all rational and disinterested people of one religion, but that they should *talk together every day*.

THE WORLD.—The world is a thing we must of necessity, either laugh at or be angry with; if we laugh with it, they say we are proud; if we are angry at it, they say we are ill-natured.

CONCESSION.—A man should never be ashamed to own he has been in the wrong, which is but saying in other words, that he is *wiser* today than he was yesterday.

LIBERALITY.—To relieve the oppressed is the most glorious act a man is capable of; it is in some measure doing the business of God and Providence.

THE IRISHMAN'S VISIT.—An Irish sailor once visited a city, where he said "they *copper-bottomed* the *tops* of their houses with *sheet-lead.*"

WIT.—Wit in conversation is only readiness of thought and a facility of expression; or, in a midwife's phrase, a quick conception and an easy delivery.

Unknown – "The Nailer" (*Three Songs*) (1820)

My merry gentle people,
    Pray will you list a minute,
For though my song it is not long,
    There's something comic in it.
To sing of Nails, if you'll permit,
    My sportive muse intends, Sir;
A subject which I now have pat,
    Just at my fingers' ends, Sir.

The world is a bag of Nails,
    And some are very queer ones;
And some are flats and some are sharps,
    And some are very dear ones.
We've Sprigs, and Spikes, and Sparables,
    Some little, great, and small, Sir,
Some folks love Nails with monstrous heads,
    And some love none at all, Sir.

The Bachelor's a Hob Nail,
    He rusts for want of use, Sir,
The Misers they've no Nails at all,
    They're all a pack of Screws, Sir,
The French Mounseers will get some Clouts,
    If here they chance to roam, Sir,
For Englishmen, like Hammers, will
    Be sure to drive them home, Sir.

J. S. Greene – "Roger McRoy" (*Christian Telescope*) (1827)

"The world is a vast mart for man to buy and sell in," said Roger McRoy, when he sat out in business, and he shaped his character with a reference solely to his view of life. He was honest, because he formed a valuable advantage to him in the way of trade, to secure the countenance of the solid part of the community. He was very punctual in his dealings, because it gave him customers and confidence. He was pleasant and amiable in all his intercourse with society, for by this means he obtained friends, and became popular—and he was industrious for this filled his leather purse with dollars, and plaistered over the occasional aberrations in conduct which a man of his principles occasionally suffers.

Roger soon therefore stood forth, a wonderful example of the fair structure that may be built upon a purely selfish foundation.—And he became proud and void of the estimation in which he was held, while he still labored to garnish over his system of morals by a thousand little acts, which to a superficial observer, seemed to spring from disinterested motives, from pure and innate benevolence. His acts of charity were occasionally blazoned abroad, and indeed he was not backward in blowing his own trumpet on well selected occasions. But people who only looked to the exterior, and very few are able to look much deeper, set him down as a remarkably clever, good sort of a man—and so he was as far as his general intercourse with others was concerned. He was just as good as policy required him to be.

Old Meadows, who lived on the farm hard by Mr. McRoy's, and

Daniel Bryan – "Miscellanea" (*The New-York Mirror*) (1827) i.

THE WORLD.— Believe me, **the world is a mighty pleasant creature, only do not expect too much from it**. In the hour of peace, of prosperity, and relaxation, seek the world; in moderation, taste of it as you would of a strong cordial; but lose not the remembrance that it turns bitter on the lees: drink it not to excess, or it will lead to folly, ignominy, or death. Hope nothing from the world in the hour of sorrow. Hope little even from friends: try them not too much—it is painful to find them wanting. Trust only in that world which is not now, but which must come to all, whether they will or not. Look at the great word, written over the portal of death. Eternity—and seek your comfort there.

* * *

The late Archbishop of Bordeaux was remarkable for his tolerance and enlightened benevolence. The following anecdote will not be read without interest. "My lord," said a person to him one day, "here is a poor woman come to ask charity; what do you wish to do for her?"

"How old is she?"

"Seventy."

"Is she in great distress?"

"She says so."

"She must be relieved; give her twenty-five francs."

"Twenty-five francs, my ford, is too much, especially as she is a Jewess."

"A Jewess!"

hours of thy fortune, when, perchance, they may soften the iron hearts of thy brethren, and awaken the feelings of a father in the bosom of him who gave thee birth Secrets of deep import were long ago revealed to me, my love! and they are almost verified—but I must be brief, for my departure hastens on. Thou hast ever been very dear to me, Clara! and many a time, within these few days past, my heart hath yearned toward thee more fervently than the heart of man is wont to do, for I had often proved the depth of thy affection, and I could not bear to imagine what thy grief would be when the angel of death had summoned me away. But, Clara! thou art a Christian woman, and unavailing grief for me would wrong our little ones, and prove unacceptable in the sight of Him, who, when on earth, bestowed his blessing on such as they are. Therefore, I charge thee, think not of me when the voices of the living call upon thee to guide and counsel them." Here his voice faltered, and he paused a moment—but Clara was too deeply affected to utter a word, and he resumed, in a low, broken, hollow tone—"When I am gone, return with thy children to thy father's house; for he may forget that thou didst love me, and deal kindly by thee as in the days of thy girlhood—and **the world is a cold and a cruel place**, Clara, to the desolate widow and the fatherless. Go, then, to thy father's house, and, as thou bearest back enough of the fruits of my labours to redeem thee from the charge of penury, I trust that thy father will forget thy disobedience, and forgive the love thou hast rendered unto me." Again the dying man paused, gasping for breath journey was renewed along the river-bank; George the guide kept close by Paul's side; an hour elapsed before they exchanged words. "Young man," said the American, "I wish to warn you of the perils which lie in the path you have chosen;—you have courage and talent,—you have firm ness and presence of mind,—you but perhaps you have no wish to hear my counsel?"—"The path I am pursuing," replied Paul, "is ever present to my mind. It was resolved upon in no gay and careless hour; and, though personal insult and persecution might be pleaded as reasons for my hostility to Britain, I take my stand on the vantage-ground of love of liberty and good wishes for the happiness of the human race. When you speak to me, address me as one who has no country and no home—a citizen of the world."

"The world is a wide inheritance," replied the guide; "my love is limited to the Thirteen Provinces,—when their freedom is achieved I may have leisure to love all mankind. But let that be—of other matters I wish to speak. Are you prepared to endure all that Scotland will say of you?—she already calls you traitor,—says that you joined her enemies without cause,—attacked her ships and her shores with the sword,—used your local knowledge for the destruction of the spot where you were cradled, and burned with fire the little town where you were nursed on your mother's knee." Paul said with a faltering tongue, "Who dares to call me traitor to my face? Who dares to say that I have visited my birth-place in anger? Alas! I visited it in deep sorrow, and the tears which I shed which could not be heard by Captain Corbie or his companions. "Well, John, ye have drawn a very fair picture," said Halliday, "with a poetical touch or two in it, and if all be sweet that's sunny o't, I wish ye joy of the prospect. There's no doubt that knowledge is growing too strong for superstition with all her curb-reins, and freedom too mighty for the spirits that seek to restrain it. I have aye had a thought, that our peers and proud ones of the earth ought to put a feather the less in their bonnets, and abate their peacock airs, and reverence the humble children of the land more. Yet, I confess, I cannot well see how this blessed equality of yours can be brought about, till it pleases God to make us all of one mind as he has made us all of one mould. I doubt, John, I doubt some maun still hew wood and some maun still draw water."

"Halliday," said Paul, "ye have spoken much after my own heart,—some backs maun bear burdens, while others wear purple and gold. I hold that the three-fourths of mankind are made but a degree above the brutes, and are unfit to reason, to comprehend and feel—are fit only to be driven. **The world is like a net, some men are the corks which keep it from sinking, others are the leads which drag it to the bottom.** But here is the evil: A man rises by the force of his genius—saves his country or improves her condition—is rewarded—a coronet is placed on his head and a pension put in his pocket; and well he merits it all,—and here is my hat in my hand, and my head bowed down to one so worthy of honour. But behold his house in the third generation—in that puppy lord,—

fur id, this penny and that penny, and puttin' odds and ends together, all to no good."

"Och, then, my darlin', is id cryin' you are? Don't now, a-cuishla, don't."

"Oh, Andy, an' afther you cum round me, in the way you did, an' made me so sure iv id."

"Well, Bridge, honey—"

"It 's thrue enough what the poor misthress says; the boys, God mend 'em, says she, is all rogues: Anasthause an' myself used to think she'd be only sayin' id to keep us to the work, but it's now, I'm sarten iv id, to my sorrow."

"Hearken to me, a hudg."

"An' what 'ill Peggy Bawn say now, becase she begrudged me sich a clane boy; he made a vow, my dear, never to marry 'till Pierce Shea 'ud be doin' id along wid him; an' Pierce Shea 'ill never lay his eyes on Alley Doolin, while the world is a world, nor never take up wid ano ther afther her, that's sarten ; and so, by coorse, Andy Awling 'ill never marry Bridge Chree—Och, God forgi' you, Andy, praise be to his name fur all things, it's a grate thrial you brought on me."

To gain a certain point with his mistress, Andy had acquainted her with the vow in ques tion, but seeing her take it to heart more griev ously than he expected, or, indeed, could bear, he now resolved to patch up the matter. "Musha, Bridge, what signifies a small little twelvemonth, afther all?"

“And you take your game to the ladies at the Lodge, I suppose.”

“What ladies?”

“Lady Cleveland and Miss Percy. You may as well be honest, Langton, and tell the truth for once in your life at least. I know you have been at the Lodge.”

“Well, Percy, my good fellow, there's no hiding any thing from you: I will tell you the truth; I have been at the Lodge; and I would have told you so before, but you are so confoundded hot. But to speak plainly, I thought it most prudent to let my going there be kept a secret; the world is so censorious.

“Very considerate, I protest,” said Percy, reddening with vexation.

“Why, I could not be too particular, in this case; for you know, Seyton, or you might have heard, that her ladyship was spoken lightly of before on account of her attention to me.”

“Fool,” cried Percy, turning from him with a look of unconcealed contempt; and clapping the door of the little parlour after him, as he entered it. “Surely,” said he to himself, “I have nothing to fear from this wretch:—Flora must despise, detest him. I will return to London, and wait if I can with patience till she return also.”

He ordered his horse, and immediately went back to London. As he entered his aunt's house, he thought that the servant who opened the door for him had an appearance of more than common gravity. He asked whether any thing was the matter. The man shook his head, and answered in a sorrowful tone, that Mrs. Ellars

Unknown – "Notes of a Tour in Northern Europe" (1840)

Somebody has wisely remarked that the world is like a large book, and that those who remain in one spot resemble an individual who restricts himself to the perusal of a single page. Perhaps this very apt illustration of the advantages of travel may have tempted me into an occasional summer excursion beyond "The blue confines of our island home." But in these days it is wholly superfluous to set out with any excuses for travelling, since everybody travels more or less, and takes notes into the bargain. When Tom Coryat published his "Crudities" in the seventeenth century, he was regarded as a distinguished man in society (notwithstanding all his eccentricities) because he had seen the Italians use silver forks, and the Germans eat saurkraut; but now one obtains notoriety for not having seen such things, and a great deal more so, without further prelude, we commit our travelling bag to the deep.

A journey to the North of Europe ought not to be commenced later than the end of June, or the beginning of July, if the tourist be desirous of enjoying the advantages of genial temperature, verdant scenery, and almost un interrupted daylight; yet, although I was perfectly aware of that fact, I lingered irresolutely until the middle of August before I found myself on board the Hamburgh steamer, only provided with a passport, portmanteau, and companion,—not forgetting some of those excellent introductory billets which Messrs. Herries and Farquhar so liberally furnish to their friends abroad.

warm beams are full of health and life, but whose fervid rays dry up every green thing. Related to this excessive zeal, is a false, over-acting, ill judged and troublesome philanthropy. The fountain of true philanthropy is pure, and deep, and quiet, and its streams go forth smoothly and silently; while that of false is shallow, and disturbed, and impure, and its streams bubbling and noisy. A too officious friend is almost as dangerous as an avowed enemy; and I apprehend the cause of temperance has too often found it so. I am afraid there are too many zealots in the world. I will not judge their motives, but I do believe society has quite as much to fear as to hope from them. The world is like a spring which cannot be strained be yond a certain point, without injuring its powers, or endangering a forcible reaction. Take care then lest you hazard this reaction.

Let your exertions in the cause in which you have engaged, be strong and persevering. Put forth all your influence in its favor, but look that your zeal be not in judicious and troublesome. There is such a thing as wearying out people's patience by our officious endeavors even in a good cause, and this done, all our influence is at an end. Always bear in mind that there are times and seasons for all things. Establish among your selves such regulations as may be necessary to preserve you against intemperance, and let them be such as you mean strictly to adhere to. I hope not an individual will add his name as a member of this society, except with the firm intention of abiding implicitly by its regulations. Remember it is punished, and virtue rewarded. Granted. But will the greater number of readers take notice of these punishments and rewards? Are not their minds carried to something else? Can it be imagined, that the art with which the author inspires the love of virtue can overcome that crowd of thoughts which sway them to licentiousness? To be able to inculcate virtue by so leaky a vehicle, the author must be a philosopher of the first rank. But in our age we can find but few first-rate philosophers.

Avoid such performances, where vice assumes the face of virtue; seek wisdom and knowledge without ever thinking you have found them. A man is wise while he continues in the pursuit of wisdom; but when he once fancies that he has found the object of his enquiry, he then becomes a fool. Learn to pursue virtue from the man that is blind, who never makes a step without first examining the ground with his staff.

The world is like a vast sea, mankind like a vessel sailing on its tempestuous bosom. Our prudence is its sails, the sciences serve us for oars, good or bad fortune are the favourable or contrary winds, and judgement is the rudder; without this last, the vessel is tossed by every billow, and will find shipwreck in every breeze. In a word, obscurity and indigence are the parents of vigilance and œconomy; vigilance and œconomy, of riches and honour; riches and honour, of pride and luxury; pride and luxury of impurity and idleness; and impurity and idleness again produce indigence and obscurity, Such are the revolutions of life." Adieu.

Mrs. T—— - "Verses" (*The Scots Magazine*) (1766)

The Americans are jolly dogs,
    And live upon the spoil;
Then who the devil would stay here?—
    I'm sure it's not worth while,
        For a begging we must go, &c.

Farewell to Peace and Plenty,
    Which us'd to bless this isle:
Farewell to all our heroes,
    Who rais'd us by their toil,
        When a fighting they did go, &c.

The world is like a whirligigg,
    So things fall out by chance,
America is England,
    And England will be France,
        When to America we go, &c.

Tune: Made as she fat with her husband fishing at a water-mill.

See'st thou, my dear, this water-mill!
    Then listen, whilst I show
What sage reflections thence distill,
    What lessons from it flow.

Above, with smooth and silent pace,
    The current bends its force;
Below, it runs a rapid race,
    Foams boisterous, rough, and hoarse.

So wisdom works—still, deep, and strong,
    On useful purpose bent:
Thus, folly's bubbles float along,
    In useless clamour spent.

True friendship, so—with silent care
    Comes on with real aid:

"O Balderdash" – "Letter to Christopher North" (*Blackwood's*) (1821)

MOST RESPECTED SIR,

You are well acquainted already with the purport of the subjoined and forth coming epistles, as well as with the humble individual that aforetime has had the honour of writing unto you. But the world is a sharp critic, "*gravis censor*," as the old poet hath it; and I am therefore called upon to satisfy the scruples which it may feel on perusing them. And assuredly the unadvised disclosure of private letters, and private concerns, is what few can justify, much less I, that am a minister of the church, and a staunch upholder of the decencies of life. Therefore, I think I cannot shew such my disposition better, than by plainly and truly declaring the manner in which I became possessed of these curious documents, and the authority by which I now take upon me to publish them. Yet, I know there are some acute persons that will impugn ray veracity, be it ever so veraciously asserted; but, to them, and particularly to that half-pay captain, who, in his Preface to a Popish Work, I conjecture, called the Monastery, is said to ridicule the idea of documents being found in the way these were actually bequeathed unto me,—to them I reply, that the subjoined facts are true, for any thing they know to the contrary; and you have full power from me to certify them thereof. If, nevertheless, they look for proof more positive, or, to use a favourite expression of Pompey's great opponent, in his elegant work De Bell. Gall. lib. ter. p. 275. Edit. Delph. 8vo. 1794. Imprim. Lugdun.—"*certior factus*;" then, in such case, I bid them inquire for me, the Reverend Owen Owen just as little to be a Peasant; at the same time, also, I am just as indifferent about your golden mediocrity. I would be Peasant or King, the High-priest of Jupiter, or the Porter at the gate of his temple, just as it should happen. It would, I say, be altogether the same to me.

ARIST. But, after all, it must be granted, that you should prefer, tho' mistakenly, some one state to another; or you will have nothing further to desire.

THA. There is no one state preferable to another. And, tho' there should be persons who desire nothing, it is not because nothing is wanting to their station, but, because they know how to do without those things they cannot easily obtain. The world is like a fair, where the generality of people walk about, eye every thing, and cry what a number of things is here that we want! Socrates, in the same circumstances, was of a different way of thinking: what a number of things are here, said he, that I do not require! It must not, however, be thence concluded, that Socrates was in want of nothing: but, that he could, very easily, do without what was not in his power to have; whereas other men cannot put up with the loss, or absence, of such things, without reluctance and chagrin.

ARIST. You will allow, nevertheless, that, at least, in some certain stations of life, there is less to be desired than in others.

when the important labours of the harvest call the *husbandman* abroad before the day is fully risen.

After all the ardours of the sultry day, how reviving is this *coolness*! This gives new verdure to the fading plants, new vivacity to the withering flowers, and a more exquisite fragrance to their mingled scents: by this, the air also receives a new force; and is qualified to exert itself with greater activity—qualified to brace our limbs, to heave our lungs, and to co-operate with a brisker impulse in perpetuating the circulation of our blood. This I might call the grand *alembic* of nature, which distils her most sovereign *cordial*, the refreshing *dews*. In cessant heat would rob us of their beneficial agency, and oblige them to evaporate in imperceptible exhalations. Turbulent winds, or even the gentler motions of *Aurora's* fan, would dissipate the rising vapours, and not suffer them to form a coalition.—But, favoured by the stillness, and condensed by the coolness of the night, they unite in pearly drops, and create that *finely-tempered* humidity which cheers the vegetable world, as sleep exhilarates the animal.

Not unlike to these are the advantages of *solitude*. The world is a troubled ocean, and who can erect stable purposes on its fluctuating waves? The world is a school of wrong; and who does not feel himself warping to its pernicious influences? On this sea of glass, how insensibly we slide from our own steadfastness! Some sacred *truth*, which was struck in lively characters on our souls, is obscured, if not obliterated; some worthy *resolution*, which heaven that of private interest. And, hence arises the difficulty of obtaining a fair representation of facts, in times of great political animosity.

8. It should also be considered, whether there be reason to presume that the witness spoke his real judgment of the fact in question. For, there are subjects and occasions, on which even men of general veracity assume the liberty of deviating from truth; and that liberty is, though tacitly, yet so generally allowed by the world, that scarcely any loss of character is sustained thereby. **The world is a great theatre, men are players, each acting a part.** On this stage they speak rather according to their assumed character, than according to their real judgment. And though this licence is used more frequently, as to opinions, than as to the statement of facts, yet it is not strictly confined to opinions. And should we charge any man with a disregard to truth on this account, we should probably be despised for illiberality, or ignorance of the world. For the same man, when he had laid aside the mask, and retired within the circle of his private connexions, would shew that, under his real character, he felt the obligations of veracity; and would give a very different view of the fact from what he had given on the stage. And again, some persons regard it as allowable to practise a sort of *pious frauds*, on occasions which they deem important. Thus, when they think the correct knowledge of a fact with all its circumstances, would be injurious, they will so modify their relation of it, by suppressions and omissions, or even by colourings, as to convey a false idea of it. Or, when they imagine an erroneous view of the

idolater of gold; and transmitted the said idolatry, (the only religion he ever had,) together with a hand some beg inning estate, to this favourite son. Clincher set out in life animated with one single passion, the desire to be rich. To this point all the facultics of his soul, which are naturally far from the weakest, have been most strenuously devoted. He is capitally skilled in the making of bargains, and makes a great many. On this subject his maxim is, "**all the world is a cheat, and he is a fool that has no hand in the game**." To deceive the simple, to overreach even the cunning, are his constant study. He does not care for reputation; all his precaution is to keep clear of the laws against fraud. But such is his avarice that he sometimes falls into their gripe, and suffers severely for his dishonest practices; without gaining the least in ward cure of his shameful propensity to make the most he can out of every body that comes in his way. No man who knows him puts the smallest confidence in his word, as to the qualities and value of any thing he has to sell. In the shaving business he has many rivals, but no equal within a hundred miles around. When any man offers to sell him paper, he is so artful that you would think-some familiar spirit must aid him in finding out the precise degree of the seller's distress; and he feels no scruple to purchase a bond at one half of its real value in a fair monied marker. In lending money, he takes only legal interest, for fear of the laws against usury. But he has invented a trick for which the whole brotherhood of misers should honour him with a statue; I mean that if compelling the borrower to take

2.

THE WORLD IS A PHILOSOPHICAL PLACE

into politics, doubtless because it was more needed there and therefore the rewards were higher. It has been more important that the country should be developed than that it should be governed by the greatest skill. But there can be no doubt that we need all the ability we can get in our government at the present time and that we shall want, if we can get them, trained lawyers as well as economists in our legislatures. But here again the situation is different from that in England; and political life generally means giving up the law for the time and rather a falling off in legal capacity, although I should not advise any one to sleep on that consideration if he should be trying a case against Senator Hoar. In one of the most beautiful pieces of English in the world, the essay called *The Lantern-Bearers*, Mr. Robert Louis Stevenson shows us how in their hearts all men are idealists. The only criticism which I should make upon his adorable essay is that his examples find their ideals outside their daily pursuits.

George Herbert's

> "Who sweeps a room as for Thy laws,
> Makes that and th' action fine,"

has an intellectual as well as a moral meaning. If the world is a subject for rational thought it is all of one piece; the same laws are found everywhere, and everything is connected with everything else; and if this is so, there is nothing mean, and nothing in which may not be seen the universal law.

The difference between gossip and philosophy lies only in one's defence, it would be to betray their trust if they did. No, my Lords, they have another and a very different duty to perform on this occasion. They are bound not to suffer public opinion, which often prevents judgment and often defeats its effects, to be debauched and corrupted. Much less is this to be suffered in the presence of our co-ordinate branch of legislature, and as it were with your and our own tacit acquiescence. Whenever the publick mind is misled, it becomes the duty of the Commons of Great Britain to give it a more proper tone and a juster way of thinking. When ignorance and corruption have usurped the professor's chair, and placed themselves in the seats of science and of virtue, it is high time for us to speak out. We know that the doctrines of folly are of great use to the professors of vice. We know that it is one of the signs of a corrupt and degenerate age, and one of the means of insuring its further corruption and degeneracy, to give mild and lenient epithets to vices and to crimes. **The world is much influenced by names.** And as terms are the representatives of sentiments, when persons who exercise any censorial magistracy seem in their language to compromise with crimes and criminals, by expressing no horror of the one or detestation of the other, the world will naturally think that they act merely to acquit themselves in its sight in form, but in reality to evade their duty. Yes, my Lords, the world must think, that such persons palter with their sacred trust, and are tender to crimes because they look forward to the future possession of the same power, which they now prosecute, and purpose to

W. M. Patterson – *The Growing World* (1885)

What is the world, even to those who love It, who are intoxicated with the pleasures, and who cannot live without it? The world is a perpetual servitude, where no one lives for himself alone, and where, if we strive to be happy, we must kiss its fetters and live its bondage. The world is a daily revolution of events, which create in succession, in the minds of its partisans, the most violent passions, bitter hatred, odious perplexities, devouring jealousy, and grievous chagrins.

The world! it is a place of malediction, where pleasures themselves carry with them their troubles and afflictions. In the world there is nothing lasting— nor fortune the most affluent—nor friendship the most sincere—nor character the most exalted—nor favors the most enviable. Men pass their lives in agitation, projects, and schemes; always ready to deceive, or trying to avoid deception; always eager and ready to profit by the retirement, disgrace, or death of their competitors; always occupied with their fears or their hopes; always discontented with the present and anxious about the future, never tranquil, doing everything for repose, removing still further from its vanity, ambition, vengeance, luxury and avarice; these are the virtues which the world knows and esteems. In the world, integrity passes for simplicity; duplicity and dissimulation are meritorious. The most vile interest arms brother against brother, friend against friend, and breaks all the ties of blood and friendship; and it is the base motive which produces our hatred or attachments. The wants and misfortunes of a neighbor find only philosophy is vain; and that the time bestowed upon it, in our colleges and elsewhere, is only wasted, or worse than wasted, in the pursuit of a phantom that can never be reached, while it leads us away continually from the proper use of life. What men need in this world, we are told, is not speculation, but an active apprehension of the living realities with which they are immediately surrounded, and the proper practical use of these for the ends of their own existence. **The world is a fact, broadly and palpably spread out before our senses;** and our life is a fact, which we are required to turn to right account, by making the best of it for ourselves and others, in the circumstances in which we may happen to be placed. Why, then, should we occupy ourselves with things that lie wholly beyond the sphere of our actual existence, and that can only serve to disqualify us for understanding and using the world as it is? The sense of the world is sufficiently clear of itself for such as are disposed to take things just as they are, without troubling their heads about what they are pleased to call its inward spiritual constitution and design. We have had ample experiment besides of the vanity of philosophy, in the past history of its own achievements. The world has been philosophizing since the days of Pythagoras at least, and from a still earlier date, and yet to what has it come in the end? Has its philosophy made it any wiser or better? Has it accomplished any solid gain whatever for the human race? Is the world improved in any respect by the long exploded systems of Greece, by the profound lucubrations of the school men in the exist conjointly and successively, but which are so connected together that one ever contains the ground of the other. Things are connected in space and in time. By virtue of this universal connection, the world is one united whole; the essence of the world consists in the mode of this connection. But this mode cannot be changed. It can neither receive any new ingredients nor lose any of those it possesses. From the essence of the world spring all its changes. In this respect **the world is a machine.** Events in the world are only hypothetically necessary in so far as previous events have had a given character; they are accidental in so far as the world might have been directed otherwise. In respect to the question whether the world had a beginning in time, Wolff does not express himself explicitly. Since God is independent of time, but the world has been from eternity in time, the world therefore is in no case eternal in the same sense that God is eternal. But according to Wolff, neither space nor time has any substantial being. Body is a thing composed of matter, and possessing a moving power within itself. The powers of a body taken together are called its nature, and the comprehension of all being is called nature in general. That which has its ground in the essence of the world is called natural, and that which has not is supernatural, or a miracle. At the close of his cosmology, Wolff treats of the perfection and imperfection of the world. The perfection of a world consists in this, that all things, whether simultaneous or successive, exist in perfect harmony. But since everything has its separate rules, the individual must give up fundamental thought of the Pythagorean philosophy is that of proportion and harmony. This thought is, for it, both the principle of practical life, and the supreme law of the universe. The Pythagorean cosmology regards the universe as a symmetrically ordered whole, uniting harmoniously in itself all the differences and antitheses of being, — a view which is most clearly expressed in the Pythagorean doctrine, that all cosmical bodies or spheres (including the earth) revolve in fixed orbits about a common middle point, a central fire, from which light, warmth, and life stream forth into the whole universe. The more strictly metaphysical confirmation of this idea, that **the world is a whole, harmoniously articulated in accordance with fixed forms and proportions**, is the Pythagorean doctrine of number. Through number alone, the quantitative relations of things, extension, magnitude, figure (triangular, quadrangular, cubic, etc.), combination, distance, etc., obtain their peculiar character ; the forms and proportions of things can all be reduced to number. Therefore, it was concluded, since without form and proportion nothing can exist, number must be the principle of things themselves, as well as of the order in which they manifest themselves in the world. The accounts of the ancients are not at one as regards the question, whether the Pythagoreans supposed number to be an actual, material, or a purely ideal principle of things, *i.e.*, the archetype in accordance with which everything is formed and ordered. Even the expressions of Aristotle seem to regarding natural phenomena, cannot in this case be admitted, because the questions raised do not relate to the nature of things, but are necessarily originated by the nature of reason itself, and relate to its own internal constitution. We can now establish this assertion, which at first sight appeared so rash, in relation to the two questions in which reason takes the greatest interest, and thus complete our discussion of the dialectic of pure reason.

If, then, the question is asked, in relation to transcendental theology; *first*, whether there is anything distinct from the world, which contains the ground of cosmical order and connection according to general laws? The answer is, *Certainly*. For **the world is a sum of phenomena;** there must therefore be some transcendental basis of these phenomena, that is, a basis cogitable by the pure understanding alone. If, *secondly*, the question is asked, whether this being is substance, whether it is of the greatest reality, whether it is necessary, and so forth? I answer that *this question is utterly without meaning*. For all the categories which aid me in forming a conception of an object, cannot be employed except in the world of sense, and are without meaning, when not applied to objects of actual or possible experience. Out of this sphere, they are not properly conceptions, but the mere marks or indices of conceptions, which we may admit, although they cannot, without the help of experience, help us to understand any subject or thing. If, *thirdly*, the question is, whether we may not cogitate this being, which is distinct from the world, in analogy with the objects of may be untenable as it was understood by dogmatists, yet there is a truth in supernaturalism which will remain true forever.

Those who see in the facts of nature only matter in motion, will naturally be surprised at the fact that a cosmos with living and morally aspiring beings can develop out of it. A deeper insight into the conditions of nature reveals to us that **the world is a well regulated cosmos,** having its own definite and immutable laws, and these laws are realities as much as material things. They are not concrete entities, but they are real, nevertheless, and indeed of greater importance than the existence of sense-perceptible objects. The cosmos is not only an enormous mass of innumerable atoms, and molecules, and masses of suns and stars, but its finer texture shows that down into its most delicate details it is a wonderful systematic whole, full of life and consistency, and possessing an out spoken and clearly intelligible character. The world possesses objectivity, i. e., it is a reality independent of what we think it to be. **The world is not as we think it to be,** but we must think the world as it is, and our duty is to act accordingly.

These are the plain facts of science which even the man who has no idea of science must mind. Only those creatures can in the long run of evolution survive who act according to the truth. Thus, the truth became embodied in moral rules, even before science could deduce or explain them. Religion is a revelation in so far as it is an anticipation of certain truths which were at the time of their invention still uncomprehended. Religious ideas, accordingly, had have sung, though he could hardly have written, the Song of Little Sister Death. But it is to be noticed that, though he recognized frankly the law of change, the idea of progress never entered into his head. **The world is like a river; true, but it is like a river that flows upwards.** But in the eyes of Marcus, though nothing endures, yet there is nothing new under the sun. The world is like an interminable procession of ants, like a stage army that marches out at one door and in. at another. Endless change, yet wearisome monotony. The lesson is that of Ecclesiastes, 'Vanity of vanities, and all is vanity.' How can you fix your heart on one of a flock of birds driven past by the wind? Let them go, and be ready to go with them when the hour strikes. Yes, we might say, but, O Marcus, are we not to make the world better? Are we set here merely to endure boredom as best we can?

Christians were saved from this dull melancholy partly by the Epistle to the Hebrews, and the Bible history generally, still more by the belief in immortality. They were not so unscientific as Marcus probably thought.

But the theology of Marcus is really his psychology. It is the reflex of his view of human nature; with this it begins, and to this it returns. In his view of the world there is really nothing better than man.

Man consists of three parts, flesh, spirit, and intelligence. By the first two, which are material, he is akin to beasts, plants, and inanimate nature, entangled, like them, in the iron laws which made in these young men, and questioned them as to the manner in which they had spent their time. Frank's history was soon told, but Simon was ashamed of his case being known. When the gentleman learned the cause, he said, "Oh! foolish Simon, had you but reflected that all the movements in the organic structure of man and beast were totally subject to the NERVES OF WILL; and that all the tendons, muscles, &c, are but the instruments formed to obey them, then you *might* have gained the prize." The youth replied," I thought the same force which is good for the fingers were equally beneficial to the legs." To which the gentleman rejoined, "You are quite right—the power which moves the fingers sets the legs in motion: but what is that power? — your machine sets your legs in motion, and the springs you employed unnaturally stretched, and therefore weakened, the tendons, which prevented the legitimate action of your joints, whilst the NERVES OF WILL lay dormant all the while." Simon then said, "Would that I had never read of *the Chirogymnast*, for then I should not have been so deluded." To which the sage replied, "Young man, **the world is like a stream of water which rushes onwards and pauses not to ask the reason why.** Take not for granted all you see, hear, or read, but commune with yourself, before you give ought credence; things on the surface seem at times so favorable that even the wisest men must exert their utmost reason, or be themselves deceived. I am an admirer of gymnastic exercises; but, I fear, this new invention you have named is opposed to them, for, in all the gymnastic exercises end in the limit of the world's equilibrium; but the system of the world's work unlimited within the limit of equilibrium, there is no limit to the world as an equilibrium of creative work. If the world's system of work is true, the limited world equilibrium or idea of creative work that is unfolded to us as in our idea is the greater truth, for it becomes a tangible entity from which all fate and chance is eliminated, is the world of reality as a purposive unity of creative work. **The world is truth with system wherein man's system and truth is a related part.**

It is thus again, by another route, we have reached the conclusion that the world is an idea of creative work, a constructive system of living truth. Heretofore we have conceived the problem that we are a limited idea and system of truth in the unlimited world idea and truth, but it will no longer answer, for the world is a limited work with its system of truth, and as such can make no mistake's, is always the limit of truth, while our truth and work is unlimited. Indeed, if our unlimited truth and world could attain the limit of the world truth and work we would be the world. This limited equilibrium of creative work as an ever-present unity is the world idea, or God; and man's idea of the world an unlimited equilibrium, is the system and measure of relation between God and man. This is the physical, the scientific statement and elucidation of the system of the world problem with system, the terms of which we find in the ever-present world equilibrium of relation that is known to us in our idea; indeed is the only world we developed intuitions are often found to make correct predictions of events. The Yogis are persons of this description. Their peculiar knowledge is certainly not the result of any study of astrological works. We also find another class of men who imitate these men and also make striking *statements*. Birmingham gold is often taken for sterling gold; German silver for pure silver; and we have a variety of inferior stones, white, red and green that are often mistaken for diamonds, rubies and emeralds. **The world is full of this dual character of things.** Every department of true knowledge has its inferior counterpart; and so we have a number of men who, possessing no occult powers, but securing the help of a few elemental spirits, practise imposition on the ignorant public. But **the world is not without a touchstone to detect the hollowness of their pretensions**: these men will give you a few correct particulars regarding remote past events, a great deal of particulars regarding present events, one or two particulars regarding the immediate future, and no particulars at all about the distant future. I have known these men and tested the truth of their statements. These men pretend to be astrologers. Some of them carry no books at till and make amazing statements touching past events in prose and verse in an extempore sing-song fashion arid without the least effort, even though the questioner is a perfect stranger; while others show you some huge antique cadjan book and pretend to read from its pages. This was exactly the way in which Col. Olcott's questions were recently answered by the Brahmin astrologer who pretended

N. Chidambaram Iyer – Introduction to *Brihat Jataka* (1885) ii.

planets together form a body of executive officers charged with the duty of rewarding and punishing humanity for their past karma by the command of the Most High, who at the same time allows each man the chance to improve his own condition by making him a free agent in many matters. A man is whipped for theft by the order of the Magistrate. He suffers for his karma—the deed of theft. But the whipping officer is an active agent. Take another instance: A man does a piece of valuable service to the state; the sovereign commands a local officer to invest the person with the order of knighthood; the officer obeys; the officer no doubt is an active agent, though the honor was the immediate effect of the person's services. We therefore hold that planets not only indicate human destinies, but bring about such destinies. **The world is a mixed field of honor, of punishment and of probation**. And the planets are the rewarding and chastising officers, and meddle in no way when man exercises his free will within its own sphere.

The same idea might be represented in another way : planetary activity is the total activity of a number of forces, some for good and some for evil, and while a man's karma leads him into the one force or the other, there are other forces by a knowledge of which man may benefit himself, though it may not be his lot to be drawn into any of them by his past karma. If this were not the correct view of the part played by the planets, a large portion of the science of astrology, in which man is advised to avail himself of such and such planetary positions for particular purposes, would become useless.

of Art are not so strange, but that those of Nature are much stranger; and that in the way of *Mechanism*, tho' partly our Ignorance of them, and partly our familiarity with them, makes us less sensible of it. The Works of Nature are so admirable, that 'tis one of our great Studies to contemplate them, and our Philosophy to understand them. And yet these Works, as excellent and as admirable as they are, must be confess'd, at least in great part, to be mechanically perform'd. **The World is a great *Machine*, and goes like a Watch**, and the several Bodies that compose its System are, as to their constituent Principles (for I speak not of their efficient Cause) mechanically made and laid together, and must be in like manner resolv'd and accounted for. And so as to the Operations of Nature, as great and as strange as they are, they proceed ordinarily from Mechanism, the wise disposition of Matter and Motion, and then do we understand them most perfectly, and philosophize upon them with best Satisfaction, when we can resolve them into their *Natural*, that is, their *Mechanick* Causes. For tho' other Principles (fit rather to amuse than instruct) have been pretended, yet I doubt not but that the true Reason after all why the Loadstone draws Iron, or why Salt preserves Bodies from Corruption, or why the Air dissolves them, why Rubarb purges, or why the Fruit of the Quince-tree binds, why Opiates still and quiet the Spirits, or why Coffee disperses them, *&c.* I say, the true and only Reason of these Appearances (tho' not always very easy to find) must be such as is taken from the specific Contexture of these Bodies, and the di-

Unknown – "Allegories" (*Athenium*) (1820)

Human thoughts are like the Planetary System, where many are fixed, and many continue for ever unintelligible; or rather like meteors, which generally lose their substance with their lustre.

1. The understanding is like the Sun, which gives light and life to the whole intellectual world; but the memory regarding those things only that are past, is like the Moon, which is new and full, and has her wane by turns.

2. **The world is a sea; and life and death are its ebbing and flowing.** Wars are the storms which agitate and toss it into fury and faction. The tongue of its enraged inhabitants are then as the noise of many waters. Peace is the calm which succeeds the tempest, and hushes the billows of interest and passion to rest. Prosperity is the Sun whose beams produce plenty and com fort. Adversity is a portentous cloud impregnated with discontent, and often bursts in a torrent of desolation and distraction.

3. Wit is like a lily; the one is as pleasing to the ear as the other is to the eye. Wit naturally fades, and if timely gathered soon withers and dies.

4. On the Tower of Ambition hangs the dial of Industry, where the Sun of good Fortune marks the time and progress of Friendship on the figure of Ambition.

5. Every man may learn the elements of Geography, which is the no blest science in the world, from an attention to the temperature of his own mind. Melancholy is the North Pole — Envy the South Pole — Choler the Torrid Zone — Ambition the Zo-

demonstrated of some particular line, is in the conclusion applied to one that is universal, and this true line could be no otherwise signified to the learner than by a material description.

The certainty of axioms is, indeed, in a measure obvious to every one. For what more evident than that nothing exists of which it is possible, at the same time, to affirm and deny any circumstance of being? Indeed, so illustrious and indubitable is the light of this axiom, that in any demonstration we are ashamed to assign it the place of an assumption. It would almost seem prolix and superfluous, since there is nothing more manifest and certain; and yet there are cafes in which it is necessary to rank it among assumptions. And these take place whenever the intention is to conclude the existence of something as true, and of its opposite as false. Thus, for instance, in the demonstration that the world is finite, we assume this principle, and then reason follows:

> Bound and infinite cannot be at the same time affirmed and denied of any *body*:
>
> The world is a body:
>
> Therefore the world is not at the same time finite and infinite.

And in this genus of demonstration, the major proposition ought always to assimilate with the conclusion. But the above axiom is not the only one obvious, for the following possesses equal certainty; that of everything which exists, either affirmation or negation is true. This axiom is of great use in demonstrations leading to an ab-

Joel Giles – "An Oration Delivered before the City Authorities of Boston in the Tremont Temple" (1848)

In Eastern fable, **the world is a harp.** Earth, air, fire, water, life, death, and mind, are its seven strings. When breathed upon by the gentle winds, its music is love and peace. But, at set times, a mighty angel flies through the heavens, and strikes this harp, and its quivering strings send forth those ever-recurring pulsations of good and evil, which characterize the destiny of man. At one time, there are tempests, and floods, and earthquakes in divers places; at another, the earth becomes as ashes, and the heavens as brass, — the silver cord is loosed, and the golden bowl is broken at the fountain, — destruction wasteth at noon day, and the mourners go about the streets. Anon, the grass springs up, the fields blossom, the flocks cover the hills like morning clouds, children look out at the windows, and laughter rings again upon the glad ear of Hope. Then, suddenly, we have wars and rumors of wars; — mischief upon mischief, rumor upon rumor, and distress of nations with perplexity. But at last the silver trumpet sounds, and Liberty is proclaimed throughout all the land, unto all the inhabitants thereof; and beautiful upon the mountains are the feet of him that bringeth good tidings, that publisheth peace.

Such is the fable. The moral is plain. The course of time is marked by recurrent eras; those points of light in the darkness of the past, which shed on the present, visions of the future, and around which are grouped the great men, the noble acts, and the disappointed hopes, of our race.

Time is full of eras. Every nation, family, and heart even,

justly to know nothing else, seem to fancy they earn a right to know human nature exclusively. Let none such be trusted in their judgements upon any one, not even on themselves always.

* * *

There are certain writers of works of fiction, who seem to delight in playing at cup and ball as it were with vice and virtue. Is it *right* you thought you saw? you find it to be *wrong* : *wrong*? presto! it has become *right*. Their hero is always a moral prodigy, usually profligate, often murderous, not seldom both; but, whether both or either, always virtuous. Possessing, as they inform us, an excellent understanding, anxious, as he is evermore assuring us, at whatever cost to do right, he is continually falling into actions atrocious and detestable; not from the sinfulness of human nature, not from carelessness or presumption or rashly dallying with temptation; but because **the world is a moral labyrinth, every winding in which leads infallibly to monstrous evil**. Such an entanglement of circumstances is devised, as God in his good ness never permits to occur, except perhaps in extraordinary times to extraordinary men: into these the hero of the story is thrown headlong; and every foul and bloody step he takes, is ascribed to some amiable weakness or noble impulse well deserving our sympathy and affection.

And what fruits do these creative geniuses bring us from their wilderness of horrors ? They seduce us into a pernicious belief that sentiment and duty are irreconcilable, and thus they hypothetically the subordinate powers. This, however, is not because the superior are in want of the inferior powers to their subsistence, but, on the contrary, the body is not able to participate of the more excellent, unless it previously participates of the subordinate powers. Thus the body cannot participate of the irrational without a previous participation of the vegetative power; nor of the rational power, without a participation of both these. For, since it is necessary that no form should perish, lest the universe should be imperfect; for **the world is a plenitude of forms**; and it is impossible that sublunary natures should remain numerically the same, since they are generable and corruptible;—hence these, also, participate of perpetuity, as far as they are able, since all things desire eternity, or the first perpetuity, as their proper principle. And each individual participates of this according to its own measure. Hence, also, terrestrial natures, not being able to be numerically perpetual, each of them participates of perpetuity, by generating a being like itself. And this work of nature, viz. for every vital being to generate another like itself, is what nature proposes to herself as her principal scope. Since, therefore, we require generation, but the generative power subsists in a definite magnitude, on this account we require increase. Since, also, increase is produced through nutriment, we are in want of the nutritive power; and hence, both we, and irrational animals, participate of physical powers; so that when we energize according to these powers, we energize as plants; but when according to anger and desire, we energize as irrational

3.

THE WORLD IS A SPIRITUAL AND RELIGIOUS PLACE

may brag of; but is there not also great practical pride, though deep-hidden, only the deeper-seated? So shy a man can never have been popular. We figure to ourselves, how in those days he may have played strange freaks with his independence, and so forth: do not his own words betoken as much? "Like a very young person, I imagined it was with Work alone, and not also with Folly and Sin, in myself and others, that I had been appointed to struggle." Be this as it may, his progress from the passive Auscultatorship, towards any active Assessorship, is evidently of the slowest. By degrees, those same established men, once partially inclined to patronise him, seem to withdraw their countenance, and give him up as "a man of genius": against which procedure he, in these Papers, loudly protests. "As if," says he, "the higher did not presuppose the lower; as if he who can fly into heaven, could not also walk post if he resolved on it! But **the world is an old woman, and mistakes any gilt farthing for a gold coin; whereby being often cheated, she will thence forth trust nothing but the common copper.**"

How our winged sky-messenger, unaccepted as a terrestrial runner, contrived, in the meanwhile, to keep himself from flying skyward without return, is not too clear from these Documents. Good old Gretchen seems to have vanished from the scene, perhaps from the Earth; other Horn of Plenty, or even of Parsimony, nowhere flows for him; so that "the prompt nature of Hunger being well known," we are not without our anxiety. From private Tuition, of the wisdom of the Blessed Buddha, I made up my mind to go to Rajagaha and reap the benefits of his instruction."

Sudatta took leave of his friends and joined Chandra, the gambler, on his way to Rajagaha, and, remembering a wish once uttered by his father-in-law, he took with him the palm-leaf manuscript of the Katha-Upanishad.

While they were travelling together on the highroad, Chandra said: "Deep is the wisdom of the Perfect One. He teaches that existence is suffering, and my experience confirms the doctrine. Pessimism is indeed the true theory of life."

"What do you mean by Pessimism?" interrupted Sudatta.

"Pessimism means that the world is bad," replied Chandra; and he continued: "The world is like a lottery in which there are few prizes and innumerable blanks. We can see at once how true it is that life is not worth living by supposing a wealthy man buying all the chances in a lottery in order to make sure of winning all the prizes. He would certainly be a lower. Life is bankrupt throughout; it is like a business enterprise which does not pay its expenses."

"My friend," said the Brahman, "I perceive that you are a man of experience. Am I right in assuming that, being a gambler, you had for a time an easy life until you met another gambler better versed in trickery than yourself, who cheated you out of all your possessions?"

"Indeed, sir," said the gambler, "that is my case exactly; and now I travel to the Blessed One, who has recognised the great truth of snares. Company is a snare,—recreations are snares,—oaths are snares,—riches are golden snares,—*Opes irritamenta malorum.* The apostle speaks of "the lust of the flesh, the lust of the eyes, and the pride of life," 1 John ii. 16. The lust of the flesh is beauty,—the lust of the eye is money,—the pride of life is honour; these are the natural man's trinity. *In munda splen dor opum, glorias mqjestas, voluptatum illecebrce, ne amore Vei nos astrahunt.* The world is a flattering enemy; whom it kisses, it oft betrays; it is a silken halter; the pleasures of the world, like opium, cast men into the sleep of security. Lysimachus sold his crown for a draught of water: so many part with heaven for the world. It is an ensnaring world: the king of Armenia was sent prisoner to queen Cleopatra in golden fetters,—too many are enslaved with the world's golden fetters. The world bewitcheth Demas, 2 Tim. iv. 10. One of Christ's own apostles was caught with a silver bait. It is hard to drink the wine of prosperity, and not be giddy. Thus the world, through our innate corruption, is evil, as it is a snare, 1 Tim. vi. 9., "They that will be rich, fall into temptation, and a snare." If an angel were to live here, there were no danger of the world's ensnaring him because he hath no principle within to receive the temptation, but we have a corrupt principle that suits with the temptation, and that makes us always in danger.

It is an evil world as it is a discouraging world. It casts scorn and reproach upon them who live virtuously. What will you be holier than others, wiser than your ancestors ? The world deals with makes us believe it will satisfy our Desires, and it doth but increase them; it makes us believe it will stay with us, and it *takes Wings*, Pro. 23. 5.

7. It is an evil world, as it is a disquieting World. 'Tis full of Trouble, *John* 16. 33. **The World is like a Bee-hive; when we have tasted a little Honey, we have been stung with a thousand Bees.** St. *Basil* was of Opinion that before the Fall, the Rose did grow without Prickles; but now, every sweet Flower of our Life hath its Prickles. There are many Things cause Disquiet; Loss of Friends, Lawsuits, Crosses in Estate: Relations are not without their Troubles; some are troubled that they want Children, others troubled that they have Children; the World is a vexing Vanity. If man be poor, he is despised by the Rich; if he be rich, he is envied by the Poor. If we do not find it an ensnaring World, we shall find it an afflicting World: it hath more in it to wean us than tempt us. **The World is a Sea, where we are tossed upon the surging waves of Sorrow, and often in Danger of shipwrack;** the world is a wilderness, full of fiery Serpents. [what Storms of Persecution are raised against the Righteous? 2 *Tim*. 2. 12] The wicked are *Briars*, Mic. 7. 4. where Christ's Sheep lose some of their golden Fleece. Then, had not we need Pray, Lord, deliver us from being hurt by this evil world? why should we love the World? Tho' we are commanded to love our Enemies, yet this Enemy we must not love , 1 *John* 2. 15. *Love not the World.*

I have been all this while opening the first Sense of this

Tukaram – Poetry, ~1640 (Trans. J. Nelson Fraser 1909) i.

220

Speech cannot describe it, though you should utter all the words to our satisfaction. God's body is as it were a mirror, where each may see his own form. Infinite is the ripe crop that faith alone produces. Tukā is embarrassed by the heap of corn and sits dividing it out.

221

You have created amusing games to soothe your eyes with watching them; apart from that end, we all know what **the world is—a wooden tiger and a wooden cow!** There is unity at the bottom, but he has set an amusement afoot; he has made one light into many. Tukā says, There is no real form in the mirror, the reflection serves as an amusement.

222

When you have the evidence of your mind, why do you need public opinion? You have your own advantage within yourself. The true faith you should hold is your own reflection that God pervades all, within and without you. With pure faith on your side, you need not abandon the world; the truth will come to light anywhere. The man who has tasted inward sweetness values it; he cares no more for outward show. Tukā says, Pure faith brings this about; God will belong to those who possess it.

223

Time devours all this visible world; all things are ever passing from birth to destruction. As the sprout lies hidden in the seed, so is the infinite one the last resort of all things. Tukā says, Sound is resolved

Tukaram – Poetry, ~1640 (Trans. J. Nelson Fraser 1909) ii.

888

The servants of Hari are like Hari; free from fear, desire, anxious care and hope, they heed not the world; they are girded up with the strength of devotion. They have clasped his feet and abandoned the world; they need not honour perishable goods. His name in their throats is a draught of nectar; they need nothing else. There is infinite room for compassion within him; **the world is like a deep sea.** The grip of lust and anger cannot be loosened; these are demons that press us into their service. They are strong enough to vanquish death; humble enough to retire before all men; generous enough to give themselves away; possessing all accomplishments, they claim no knowledge. **The world is their servant**; liberation waits their time. They send prosperity and perfection wandering; yea, the people of Vishnu will not touch them. They look on birth and death as a dream; they cannot tell their own from what is other men's. Tukā says, With increasing delight I tell the story of their love.

889

Such are the saints who meet us on this path that the fetter of the world is broken at the sight of them; they are ever filled with the joy of true mind and true being; we shall honour them as hallowed sources of liberation. Faith is their all-sufficing principle; nothing breaks their repose; they crush the spirit of infidelity. By their mercy to all creatures they destroy the root of hatred; they treat all as brothers,—friend, foe, or child of their own. Purify your from a being who caused the precious blood of the Son of God to be shed, as the only means of redemption, to desire that he will love that infinite goodness which so abundantly freely loved him, and cleave unto his idols no longer. Believe me, my child, that he who sets up anything in his heart but God, is as truly an idolator as he who makes any carved or graven image to worship it. It is not merely the bended knee, it is the idolatrous heart which worships and serves the creature more than the Creator. O that we would but consider what this world is, to which we cling with such tenacity; and what this life, which is wasted in a vain search after happiness, which here is not to be found: that we would but remember how both alike are perishing; **the world is flying from us**, and we are passing from the world: we should then perceive how idle it is to spend our time in snatching at slippery icicles, which are perpetually sliding from our grasp, and which, were it otherwise, we can grasp but for a moment. Could we even be sure that the icicle would not melt in our hand, yet the hand itself must soon become as cold as that which it contains, and loose its hold forever. And is this a world to seek after; to rest in; to cling to; to set our affections upon? O well said the Preacher, 'Vanity of vanities, all is vanity!' Yes! all; the pursuits, the pleasures, the business, the hopes, the fears, the joys, the sorrows, of the unregenerate man, all alike are vanity. Yes! all is vanity which brings us not a step nearer to our final rest : all is vanity which casts a veil over our hearts, and keeps us from the fear and the love of God. All is vanity which says, peace, even to the natural one who was early torn from you, must I declare, that the path you are following is the path of sin? Alas! I must: for I cannot deceive myself, and I dare not deceive you. Is it not sin to forget the Lord who bought you? does the round of pleasure leave you any time for the consideration of your spiritual interests? does it permit you to 'commune with your own heart and in your chamber, and be still?'—On the contrary, do you not feel solitude to be as an enemy, setting your faults before you in their most hideous forms, and do you not therefore fly from it?—My poor girl," continued Mrs. Ellars, seeing that Flora was too much affected to speak, "I do not mean to upbraid, but to entreat you; to point out to you that the world is beset with snares, into which you must fall, if you seek not the guidance of an Almighty hand. I must not, now that I am about to leave you, probably for ever, do the work of the Lord deceitfully. I must faith fully represent to you the danger which yon appear not to dread; lest at the day of final account your blood should be required at my hand. Turn not then, I beseech you, away from Him that speaketh to you from heaven; take for your guide that word in which he speaks to you, as a father to an erring child, as much in pity as in anger. Pray, Flora, pray for His grace: 'watch and pray that you enter net into temptation.' Give me, before I die, the joyful, transporting, hope, that our separation is but for a season, and that we shall spend an eternity together."

When Flora could speak, she expressed the warmest gratitude to her aunt for her advice, and promised to follow it. "And yet," said accord to his throne, and praise him for all the wonders he hath done, for all the goodness he hath evinced towards me: towards *me* who am not worthy of the least of all the mercies he hath bestowed upon me. I wish to tell you that now I am passing from this world, my spirit is no longer weighed down by despair. I wish to tell you now at this moment, a moment when all the delusion of outward things is seen, and cannot be hid; I wish to tell you what are my views of this perishing existence. O! I have no words to tell its utter nothingness in my eyes; were I to describe it by the least substantial of all visible things, I would say it is a shadow. But it is less even than a shadow; for a shadow will follow you while you remain on earth, and the enjoyments of the world fly off long before. O! my friends, to you I need not say it, the world is a worthless possession. To you I need not say it, for you already feel it to be so: but I will say it, that you may know, that he who was so long the slave of its vain enchantments, feels it too. Yes, I can truly say, that I who have so long walked in the desire of my heart, and in the sight of my eyes, am now,—'in all these things, more than conqueror, through Christ, who loved me.' Who loved me: oh! what transcendent good ness, that a vessel of wrath, fitted only to destruction, should be made a vessel of mercy : o! the depth of the riches of his love! the unsearchable riches of Christ! 'Lord, what is man, that thou shouldest be mindful of him? or the son of man that thou shouldest thus visit him?' But, 'who is he that condemneth? It is Christ that died; yea, rather that is risen again, who also maketh intercession no more abate the torments of conscience, than it doth mitigate Belzebub's torments to be stiled prince of the devils. All the world's honey will not serve to allay the envenomed stingings of conscience. That is a fiery serpent, a deaf adder, that will not be charmed by all the alluring pleasures of the world. These are vain and impertinent to one whose thoughts are wholly possessed with the fear of wrath and hell, from which these cannot deliver him. When God makes a wound in the spirit, the whole world cannot make a plaister broad enough to cover it.

2. Secondly, **The World is a vain and useless thing at the hour of death.** Possibly, many of us may never conflict with the terrors of conscience, nor have that conviction of the world's vanity: but yet we must all conflict with death, that king of terrors. Suppose therefore (what must certainly once be) that we were now gasping our last, our tongues faltering, our eye-strings breaking, our limbs quivering, a dead cold and stiffness invading us; were our fouls tost to and fro upon our expiring breath, and, like wrecks at sea, sometimes cast up, and by and by sucked back again; what could stand us in stead, and make our passage happy at such a time as this? Now the foul requires the strongest, the richest cordials. Prepare it one mingled of the best ingredients the whole world can afford; cast into the cup, riches, honour, pleasure, the quintessence of all that is here desirable; yet, alas! what is all this world to a dying man who is just leaving it?

Thy wicked companions, with whom thou hast sinned

reasoning to man collective, I may seem to be imputing to a divine ordinance (for such human society is) what I have disclaimed to be imputing to man's gift of reason; but this is to mistake my meaning. **The World is a collection of individual men,** and any one of them may hold and take on himself to profess unchristian doctrine, and do his best to propagate it; but few have the power for such a work, or the opportunity. It is by their union into one body, by the intercourse of man with man, and the consequent sympathy thence arising, that error spreads and becomes an authority. Its separate units which make up the body rely upon each other, and upon the whole, for the truth of their assertions; and thus assumptions and false reasonings are received without question as certain truths, on the credit of alternate appeals and mutual cheers and *imprimaturs*.

I should like, if I could, to give a specimen of these assumptions, and the reasonings founded on them, which in my "Apologia" I considered to be "corrosive" of all religion; but before doing so, I must guard against misconstruction of what I am proposing. First, I am not proposing to carry on an argument against Dr. Fairbairn, whose own opinions, to tell the truth, I have not a dream of; but I would gladly explain, or rather complete on particular points, the statement I have before now made in several works about Faith and Reason. Next, I can truly say that, neither in those former writings nor now, have I particular authors in mind who are, or are said to be, prominent teachers in what I should call the school of the world. Such an undertaking would require a volume, instead of half

That if such Abominations were not removed, and they did repent, he *would then come quickly, and fight against them with the Sword of his Mouth.* For the Lord hateth all such Things, and punishes severally all them that give Offence; as we can be convinced of by the words of our Text, where our blessed Saviour speaketh,

FIRST, *Of Offence.*

SECOND, *Of the Punishment for Offence.*

EXPLANATION OF THE TEXT.

I. Of Offence.

As difficult as it is to walk upon the Ice without stumbling or falling, as difficult is it to live in the World without being smitten therewith: For the World is as a Coal-Pit, wherein every one that enters in, becometh smutten. There were never so many Misfortunes, Vermins and Insects in *Egypt,* but there are more Offences in the World; one offendeth the other, and the Great offend the Small. Whereof our Saviour speaketh in our Text, saying, *Whosoever shall offend one of these little Ones, which believe in me.* We have to observe here of these Words, *First*, What Offence is. And, *Secondly*, The Persons, who give or take Offence.

First, What Offence is. It is derived in the ground Text of limping, when one stumbleth against a Thing, whereof he becometh lame: and since our whole Life-time, is a continual Journey or Road; so all what causes us to stumble, or tos all on the Way of our Salvation into Sin, may be rightly called Offence.

Faciam fieri vos, I will cause ye to be made fishers of men, that is, I will provide an outward calling for you too. Our calling to this man-fishing is not good, *Nisi Dominus faciat, et fieri faciat*, except God make us fishers by an internal, and make his church to make us so too, by an external calling. Then we are fishers of men, and then we are successors to the apostles, though not in their apostleship, yet in this fishing. And then, for this fishing, the world is the sea, and our net is the Gospel.

The world is a sea in many respects and assimilations. It is a sea, as it is subject to storms, and tempests; every man (and every man is a world) feels that. And then, it is never the shallower for the calmness, the sea is as deep, there is as much water in the sea, in a calm, as in a storm; we may be drowned in a calm and flattering fortune, in prosperity, as irrecoverably, as in a wrought sea, in adversity; so the world is a sea. It is a sea, as it is bottomless to any line, which we can sound it with, and endless to any discovery that we can make of it. The purposes of the world, the ways of the world, exceed our consideration; but yet we are sure the sea hath a bottom, and sure that it hath limits, that it cannot overpass; the power of the greatest in the world, the life of the happiest in the world, cannot exceed those bounds, which God hath placed for them; so the world is a sea. It is a sea, as it hath ebbs and floods, and no man knows the true reason of those floods and those ebbs. All men have changes and vicissitudes in their bodies, (they fall sick) and in their estates, (they grow poor) and in needs to be guarded with much watchfulness and care, lest this distemper be rooted in the heart. Job sacrificed while his sons were feasting : Job i. 5, "For Job said, It may be that my sons have sinned, and cursed God in their hearts." In all these things should we use much caution.

The next particular the apostle mentions is the lusts of the eye, or covetousness. This is an evil very natural to us, and we cannot be watchful enough against the encroachments of the world. We need it in part, and we love it more than we need it. Worldliness is a branch of original sin; it is a disease we are born with. The tenth commandment, that forbids original sin, saith, "Thou shalt not covet." The best find temptations this way. We are daily conversant about the things of the world, and we receive a taint from those things with which usually we converse; we find by experience that long converse is a be witching thing. Again, **the world is a thing of present enjoyment;** we have the world in hand, and heaven in hope. The judgment of carnal men is quite different from the judgment of the word. The word of God counts the world to be but a fancy, and an apparition, and heaven to be the only substance: Prov. xxiii. 5, "Wilt thou set thine eyes upon that which is not?" It is not in comparison of better things: "And the fashion of this world passeth away," 2 Cor. vii. 31 ; but, Prov. viii. 21, "That I may cause those that love me to inherit sub stance." Heaven is the durable substance; this is the judgment of the word, but wicked men think quite otherwise. We have sensible experience of the profits of the world, ivory carver's art. Through doors of ebony one enters the dim interior where lies the tomb of the saint, under a canopy of mother-of-pearl and enclosed in walls of delicate ivory-tinted lacework that seem as frail as cobwebs, but are carved from slabs of solid stone. Nearby is the Great Mosque, a copy of the one at Mecca, and across the wide flagged courtyard stands the huge Gate of Victory, one hundred and thirty feet high and bearing on its facade the inscription "Isa (Jesus) on whom be peace, said: 'The world is a bridge, pass over it but build no house on it. The world endures but an hour, spend it in devotion.'" Just around the corner outside the gate was a large well into which skinny, white whiskered mountebanks jumped for our delectation and a little bakshish from the crenelated summit of the wall eighty feet above. We hurried back to Agra to seek shelter from the glowing mid-day sun and shortly before four were on our way to Delhi which we reached at eight. Maiden's Hotel was too full to absorb our numerous party, but at the Cecil we found agreeable and convenient quarters.

Tuesday, March 14th. Delhi. — Shahjahanabad or modern Delhi —once the capital of India under the Mogul emperors and again elevated to this dignity on the occasion of the Great Durbar in 1911 —is the sixth or seventh Delhi that has occupied this general site, so that the country for miles round about is sprinkled with the remains of countless ancient fortresses, palaces, and especially tombs, and it is an appalling task to attempt to bring order into the chaos of myths and suppositions, sackings and massacres, dates and know what God is. His Works teach us to spell; his Word teacheth us to read. The first are as it were his back parts, by which we behold him a far off: The latter shews him to us face to face. **The World is as a book consisting of three leaves**, and every leaf Printed with many Letters, and every Letter a Lecture. The leaves Heaven, the Air, and Earth with the Water. The Letters in Heaven, every Angel, Star, and Planet. In the Air, every Meteor and Soul. In the Earth and Waters, every Man, Beast, Plant, Fish, and Mineral: all these set together, spell to us that there is a God, and the Apostle faith no less though in less space, *Rom.*1.20. *For the * invisible things of him, that is, his eternal Power and Godhead are seen by the creation of the World, being considered in his Works.* And to *David, Psal.* 19.1. It is not for nothing that God hath set the Cabinet of the Universe open, but it is because he hath given us Eyes to behold his Treasure. Neither is it for nothing that he hath given us Eyes to behold his Treasure, but because he hath given us Hearts to admire upon our beholding. If we mark not the Works of God, we are like Stones that have no Eyes, wherewith to behold. If we wonder not at the Works of God, when we mark them, we are like Beasts that have no Hearts wherewith to admire. And if we praise not God for his Works, when we admire them, we are like Devils that have no Tongues wherewith to give thanks. Remarkable is the story of the poor old man, whom a Bishop found, most bitterly weeping, over an ugly Toad: being asked the reason of his Tears, his answer was, *I weep, because, that whereas God might have made me as ugly and* the evil spirit soon comes in : he comes and takes possession, and is therefore called "the God of this world:" and while we are in that state, "we walk after the course of him that worketh in the children of disobedience." We would account it a terrible thing for ourselves or any of our children to be possessed of a devil ; but what it is to be possessed of this devil thou knowest not. It is not half so bad to have a legion possess thy body, as to have but one to possess thy soul. He becomes thy God, and thou must do his work; he will tyrannize over thee. What a fearful thing therefore is this, that as soon as God departs from us and forsakes us, and we him, that the Devil should presently come in his room, and take up the heart? Mark that place in Eph. chap. II. ver. 2. "Where in times past ye walked according to the course of the world, according," &c. As soon as God leaves a man, what a fearful company assail him? They all concur together, the world, the flesh, and the Devil: these take God's place.

The world is like the tide, when a man hath the tide with him, he hath great advantage of him that rows against the tide.

But here is the Devil too. The world is as a swift current, and besides this comes the Devil and fills the heart, the "prince of the power of the air." While thou wert carried with the world thou wentest with the stream, and hadst the tide with thee; but now the Devil being come, thou hast both wind and tide; and how can he choose but run, whom the Devil drives ?

But this is not all: there must be something in thine own dispo-

St. Augustine – *The City of God* (5th c.) (trans. "JH" 1610)

After the citty, followeth the whole world, wherein the third kind of human society is resident, the first being in the house, and the second in the citty. Now **the world is as a floud of waters, the greater, the more dangerous**: and first of all, difference of language (*a*) divides man from man. For if two meete, who perchance light upon some accident craving their abiding together, and conference, if neither of them can understand the other, you may sooner make two bruite beasts, of two severall kindes sociable to one another then these two men. For when they would common together, their tongues deny to accord, which being so, all the other helps of nature, are nothing: so that a man had rather be with his owne dogge, then with another man of a strange language. But the great (*b*) westerne Babilon endeavoureth to communicate her language to all the lands she hath subdued, to procure a fuller society, and a greater aboundance of interpretours on both sides. It is true, but how many lives hath this cost? and suppose that done, the worst is not past: for although she never wanted stranger nations against whom to clad her forces, yet this large extention of her Empire procured greater warres then those, named civill and confederate warres, and these were they that troubled the soules of man-kinde both in their heate, with desire to see them extinct, and in their pacification, with feare, to see them renewed. If I would stand to recite the massacres, and the extreame effects hereof, as I might (though I cannot doe it as I should) the discourse would bee infinite. (*c*) yea but a wise man (say they) will wage none but just

Therefore it is no easy matter to persuade men to place their happiness in future expectations, which is the import of the Gospel. In pressing this, and bidding the worldlyminded abandon their beloved vices, and in telling the fatal con sequences of them, we must expect to meet, not only their scorn and contempt, but their utmost rage and impatience, to get rid of us, as so many enemies of their lusts and pleasures. This is the cross, which our Saviour prepared all his disciples to bear, who were to fight against flesh and blood, and all the allurements of the world; and it is a greater miracle, that they have had so many followers in this, than that they have gained to themselves so many enemies. The world is a strong man; and, till a stronger than he come, he will keep possession; and this is the victory, that overcometh the world, even our faith. But we are told also, that this faith is the gift of God; for all the evidence in the world will not reach the heart, unless it be prepared, like the good ground, to receive the doctrine, that is taught. Till then prejudice will create obstinacy, which will harden the heart like a rock. Under this head also you must consider many, who have not yet heard of the Gospel; and of those, who have, the far greater number have not capacity or opportunity to -examine the evidences of Christianity; but take things upon trust, just as they are taught. How many others are careless, and will not be at the pains, though they want not capacity, to enquire into the truth? These classes include the greatest part of mankind; the ignorant, the careless, the vicious, the obstinate, the ambitious, and the cova tyger or a deer, or a blanket ; he must not sit on wood, nor on the earth, nor on cloth; his back, neck, and head must be exactly erect; and he must remain motionless, keeping his eyes fixed on his nose. The act of yogŭ consists of several parts: the devotee must first with his thumbs and fingers prevent the air from issuing through his eyes, ears, nostrils, and mouth, and with his feet bind up the two other avenues of respiration. This he is to practise by degrees till he is able to exist without inspiration and respiration. He who is thus far perfected will be able to subdue his passions, and to disrelish all the pleasures of the senses. Should the mind, at any time, be again entangled in worldly attachments, the devotee must study the essential virtue of things, as, that **the world is a dream**; that God is the all in all; and thus bring back the mind to abstraction. He is next to meditate on his guardian deity according to the rules of the shastrŭ. After thus annihilating, as it were, the body and the world, he is then to fix in his mind that he and Brŭmhŭ are one, and so to settle this point as never to lose sight of it, nor return to earthly attachments.

From this state of mind arises complete pleasure; he becomes dead to food and to every other bodily want. The yogēē who has attained this state of perfection becomes emancipated in the following manner:— while he sits confining the air within his body, and closing his eyes, by the power of wisdom all his members become dead to action; he unites the energy which is lodged in the body to the soul, and they both ascend by means of the veins and

Jeremy Taylor – *Holy Living and Dying Together* (1839)

"A man is a bubble," said the Greek proverb, which Lucian represents with advantages and its proper circumstances, to this purpose ; saying, that all the world is a storm, and men rise up in their several generations, like bubbles descending *a Jove pluvio*, from God and the dew of heaven, from a tear and drop of rain, from nature and Providence: and some of these instantly sink into the deluge of their first parent, and are hidden in a sheet of water, having had no other business in the world, but to be born, that they might be able to die: others float up and down two or three turns, and suddenly disappear, and give their place to others: and they that live longest upon the face of the waters, are in perpetual motion, restless, and uneasy; and, being crushed with the great drop of a cloud, sink into flatness and a froth; the change not being great, it being hardly possible it should be more a nothing than it was before. So is every man: he is born in vanity and sin; he comes into the world like morning mushrooms, soon thrusting up their heads into the air, and conversing with their kindred of the same production, and as soon they turn into dust and forgetfulness: some of them without any other interest in the affairs of the world hut that they made their parents a little glad, and very sorrowful : others ride longer in the storm; it may be until seven years of vanity be expired, and then, peradventure, the sun shines hot upon their heads, and they fall into the shades below, into the cover of death and darkness of the grave to hide them. But if the bubble stands the shock of a bigger drop, and outlives the chances of a child, of a fence; now here he observes the *oppressed*; this he did, no doubt, as a prince, to do them justice, and *avenge them of their adversaries*, for both *feared God and regarded men*; but here he does it as a preacher, and shows,

Their troubles, *v.* 1 It grieved him (1.) To see might prevailing against right; servants, and laborers, and poor workmen, oppressed by their masters; debtors oppressed by cruel creditors, and creditors too by fraudulent debtors; tenants by hard landlords, and orphans by treacherous guardians; and worst of all, subjects oppressed by arbitrary rulers, and unjust judges. Wise men will *consider these oppressions* and contrive to do something for the relief of the oppressed. *Blessed is he that considers the poor*. (2.) To see how those that were wronged laid to heart their wrongs; and perhaps he could not forbear weeping with them. **The world is a place of weepers**; look which way we will, we have a melancholy scene, *the tears of* those that are *oppressed* with one trouble or another. (3.) To see how unable they were to help themselves. It is sad to see power misplaced, and perverted. (4.) To see how they and their calamities were slighted by all about them: they that should comfort them durst not, for fear of displeasing the oppressors, and being made their companions for offering to be their comforters. It is sad to see so little humanity among men.

2. The temptations of their condition. Being thus hardly used, they are tempted to hate and despise life, to envy the dead and wish they had never been born; *r.* 2,3. and Solomon is ready to agree with

but only the visible world. Which is so plain from the words themselves, that it is a wonder how Lactantius and St. Austin could interpret them otherwise, he making therein a question, whether this second God were [actively] sensible or no. But the same is farther manifested from other places of that Dialogue, as this for example: "*Æternitatis Dominus Deus primus est, secundus est mundus*;" The Lord of eternity is the first God, but the second God is the world.— And again, "*Summus qui dicitur Deus rector gubernatorque sensibilis Dei, ejus qui in se complectitur omnem locum, omnemque rerum substantiam*;" The supreme God is the governor of that sensible god, which contains in it all place and all the substance of things.—And that this was indeed a part of the Hermaic or Egyptian theology, that the visible world animated was a second god, and the son of the first God, appears also from those Hermaic books published by Ficinus, and vulgarly called Pœmander, though that be only the first of them. There hath been one passage already cited out of the eighth book, ζεντερος Θεός ο κόσμος, the world is a second god.—After which followeth more to the same purpose. The first God is that eternal unmade maker of all things; the second is he that is made according to the image of the first, which is contained, cherished, or nourished and immortalized by him, as by his own parent, by whom it is made an immortal animal.—So again in the ninth book, God is the father of the world, and the world is the son of God. — And in the twelfth, this whole world is a great god, and the image of a greater.

of any kind can produce vigorous exertion. Fiction may represent the union of benevolence and diseased sensibility, but real life never witnessed it. The persons who in deed and in truth do benefit the world by their labor, who here remove a weed, and there plant a flower, are, and must be cheerful; must, and will take happy views of life and its contingencies. As Christians they see, and mourn, and admit its evils; but then every moment spent in mere feeling, every sigh and every tear that does not issue in exertion, they regard as wasted. They know that **the world is a wilderness**, and that nothing but the hand of God himself, will ever change it into a fruitful field; but they know too, that in measure and in degree he will bless human efforts for its improvement; therefore, they go on and take courage. This "patient continuance in well doing" has, independent of the "glory, honor, and immortality," attached to it by the apostle, a present and consentaneous reward. I do not speak of success; that may frequently be delayed; but of the hidden, healthy happiness which they habitually experience, and which, if in one view, the effect of their active benevolence, is, in another, its cause. I am sure, if you will think over all the Christians you know, or have read of, you will be constrained to say, the happiest and the most heavenly minded, are the most active; nay, I will go further, and say, that their thoughts of heaven, if less speculative, and perhaps less vivid, are also less selfish. They realize it as a place of repose; but if God may be honored, and man benefited, they are willing to bear the heat and burden of a long life before they "rest from their la-amusements of life. But it inspires humility. It enforces dependence on divine aid; and calls forth the voice of supplication to Heaven. In a situation so critical, and where interests so important are at stake, every reasonable person must confess, that seriousness ought to temper rejoicing.

Were there in human life any fixed point of stability and rest, attainable by man; could we, at any one moment, assure ourselves that there remained no latent source of danger, either to our temporal or our spiritual state; then I admit we might lay trembling aside, and rejoice in full security. But, alas! No such safe station, no such moment of confidence, is allowed to man during his warfare on earth. Vicissitudes of good and evil, of trials and consolations, fill up his life. The best intentioned are sometimes betrayed into crimes; the most prudent overwhelmed with misfortunes. **The world is like a wheel, incessantly revolving, on which human things alternately rise and fall.** What is past of our life has been a chequered scene. On its remaining periods, uncertainty and darkness rest.

Futurity is an unknown region, into which, no man can look forward without awe, because he cannot tell what forms of danger or trial may meet him there. This we know well, that in every period of our life, the path of happiness shall be found steep and arduous; but swift and easy the descent to ruin. What, with much exertion of care and vigilance, we had built up, one unwary action may, in an evil hour, overthrow. The props of human confidence

What would those poor People do who are not susceptible of any scientific Exercises, or invincibly averse from mental Improvements, and these are the Majority? What would they do in this World, did it not afford them, and in great Abundance, those Objects, which alone, are capable of procuring them some Satisfaction? Yes; God, in his rich Benignity, appears to have taken no less Care concerning Souls of the lowest Order than those of the first Magnitude. They are all his Creatures. If to *Leibnitz* he has opened the Kingdom of Truths, if he has given to *Newton* the Expanse of the Firmament, for their Delight, he has for other Spirits prepared Objects for Complacency and Gratification suitable to their Nature; even as he feeds the meanest Insects no less than the tremendous Lion. The World is like a Museum, containing all Kinds of Curiosities, where Persons of every Taste may find Entertainment. By this Disposition it is that every thing is kept in the most beneficial Harmony; whereas nothing but Confusion, Discontent, and Enmity would follow from any other Arrangement. It is to be presumed that, whilst this Diversity in the Inclinations of Men continues, whatever other Revolutions may break forth in the Progress of Time, the World will still continue as it is; that all its Inhabitants, as at present, will find in its Oeconomy inexhaustible Sources for the respective Gratifications of which they are susceptible.

This variegated Scene of the Wisdom of God is likewise to be admired. Without an infinite Wisdom could this World have been *troubling passions, with tormenting pains, and languishing weakness, and enemies malice; with poverty and care; with losses and crosses, and shame and grief, with hard labour and studies, with the injuries and spectacles of a Bedlam world, and with fears of death, and death at last! Our enemies are our trouble, our friends are our trouble: our Rules are our trouble, and our inferiours, children and servants are our trouble: our possessions are our trouble, and so are our wants. And is all this the effect of* perfect Goodness? *And the poor Bruits seem more miserable than we! they labour, and hunger, and die at last to serve our will! we beat them, use them and abuse them at our pleasure! And all the Inanimates have no sense of any good! and which is worst of all,* ***the world is like a Dungeon of ignorance, like an Hospital of mad-men for folly and distractedness; like a band of Robbers for injury and violence, like Tygers for cruelty, like snarling Dogs for contention, and, in a word, like Hell for wickedneß.*** *What else sets the world together by the ears in wars and bloudshed in all generations! what maketh peace-makers the most neglected men? what maketh virtue and piety the mark of persecution and of common scorn? how small a part of the world hath knowledge or piety? And you tell us of a Hell for most at last. Is all this the fruit of* perfect Goodness. *These thoughts have seriously troubled some.*

Answ. He that will ever come to knowledge, must begin at the first Fundamental Truths, and in his enquiry proceed to lesser Superstructures, and reduce uncertainties and difficulties to those

John Macdonald – *Some Short Arguments and Plain Facts Shewing that the Civilization and Instruction of the Natives of India Furnish the Surest Means of Upholding the Stability of our Oriental Empire and of the Introduction and Speedy Progress of Christianity, Without Arming the Superstitious Prejudices of the Country Against That Cause: With an Alphabetic-Cipher-Table for Secret Correspondence, and a few Requisite Animadversions to Subjects Becoming Daily More Prominent and Commanding* (1820)

to make known among the distant nations, and to the uttermost corners of the earth ; and we are all called on by a sense of duty and feeling to forward as much as in us lies, the great work of fulfilling the prophecies of God. As society is constituted, contributions in money form the primary step in this great work. You expend it in public and private amusements. When not carried to excess, this may be innocent; but the comfort and satisfaction arising from after-reflection, will be inadequate to the exulting recollection of having aided in this great cause, and of having been humbly subservient in executing the decrees of Providence. We have all of us faults; and I trust we all possess virtues. The world is a system of compensations, where charity covers a multitude of sins. One of our poets has finely expressed this,—

> "—The web of Life is of mingled yarn,
> Good and ill together; our virtues would be proud,
> If our faults whipt them not; and our vices would despair,
> If they were not cherished by our virtues."

Your contributions, small and great, are well applied; but it is the permanent subscription that enables the Society to calculate on a certain result. The Ladies' Missionary Association has been very properly noticed in your excellent Report. Under the judicious patronage of Lady Kennaway, much has been done. Where all have

4.

THE WORLD IS A SCIENTIFIC PLACE

unintelligible rattle is as destitute of meaning as the rumble of the wheels on the street. But to the educated ear of the operator how wonder fully full of meaning. He interprets and translates its monotonous click into the daily history of the world, written day by day.

Now, it is a message from the king's palace. It tells the story that a great battle has been fought, a victory won, a mighty revolution is ended.

Again it is a story from a peasant's cottage, a child is sick, a funeral will be to-morrow.

The business world now speaks; prices have advanced; great fortunes are won and lost. The trained ear of the operator brings all this ceaseless clatter into contact with the mind and translates it into pages of manuscript, into columns for the newspaper, into useful information for the present, stories of the past and promises for the future.

The world is a great sounding apparatus, each thing has its own significant voice. The sky reverberates with thunder. The mountains echo. The seas roar. The brooks murmur. The winds sigh. The wild beast howls. The birds sing. The reptile hisses. The machinery hums. The car rattles and the human vocabulary has more than one hundred thousand spoken words. To the infantile ear these voices are unintelligible and terrifying. They startle, alarm and bewilder the child because they are not understood. But to the educated ear every sound is significant and full of meaning. To never did make one of the audience. Moses was like that, but he did useful work in booming the promised land.

An eminent socialist complained to me with tears in his eyes that nothing was being done for the poor. I do not agree. Not enough, certainly, but something, and every day more and more. **The world is a slow world, and Nature, like all such artisans, does her building and painting and decorating with exasperating deliberation.** Geology is slower than the South Eastern Railway. But no doubt Providence intended each of them to go at the same pace they do for our good. And it is impious to grumble. Nevertheless, if I were a sculptor called upon to design a symbolic statue of Nature, I should model a plumber. Slow, hesitating, occasionally mixing the taps and flooding the world's bathroom or exploding the gas mains in the cellars of the earth, but in the end doing the job somehow—such is the way of Nature. You cannot cinematograph the growth of the world or its rocks and trees and human beings—to study Nature you want long life and a microscope. And the only way to make out whether the tide is coming in or out is to place a mark upon the shore and wait and see. It is the same if you are travelling an unknown road—you measure your progress by the milestones. In this matter of the law and the poor, if we want to know where we are to-day and where we are likely to be three hundred years hence, the only sane way to make the experiment is to go back to what we know of things in the past, and, by measuring the progress made in bygone centuries, take heart for the morrow. That is what Sir observed. We will consider the child's reasoning under these heads. Throughout all the child's thinking, as in his imagining, he works from a personal world to an impersonal. His first ideas of cause and effect are doubtless obtained from his own movements and their results, and the sense of power appears to have its rise with the first volitions or persistent imitations in the period between four and six months. During this period the child seems to be experimenting to see what he can do. He repeats and varies a movement ad infinitum, discovering the possibilities and limitations of his movements, and at every step connecting a given movement with a certain objective result. Thus he learns that he can always get certain things by doing certain others, and has the feeling of himself as a power or cause. In all his experiences, he and others like him are, more than anything else, the causes, or movers of things. He sees very little of impersonal natural causes. This strengthens what seems to be his instinctive tendency to refer all results to a personal cause. As Sully puts it: "He starts with the amiable presupposition that all things have been hand-produced, after the manner of household possessions. The world is a sort of big house where everything has been made by somebody, or at least fetched from somewhere." "To ask who made the animals, the babies, the wind, the clouds, etc., is for him merely to apply the more familiar type of causation as the normal rule." One three-year-old girl thought that when the water spurted from the faucet, it was choking because it coughed. One child of four years thought purely a physical system with its conservation of energy in which action and reaction is equal and opposite with nothing gained or lost in con version or change, there would be no unity, no idea, no system; it would only be work without meaning or purpose, in which a unity is impossible of conception. It is thus that our science of the world fails us. This true, then **the world must be more than a scientific system of physical force or energy, for it is also a unity with its ever-present system of relation.** But what is it and where will we find it?

The unity of Nature is the unity of force, of which the system of work is the expression and measure of its being. But how can the unity of force be the measure of its system of work for all things end in the unity of force, and hence is the end of all measure; it no longer has a relation, and yet it is the measure of the system in its unity of relation. Indeed, the one denies the other, although we know they are related parts of the same truth. There must be something wrong or incomplete in our system or it would not end in this confused product. **The world is more than a unity of force; the world is a limited unity, a limited equilibrium of creative work, the system of which is the measure of its unity of relation. The world a unity of ever-present relation with limit**, is the limited equilibrium of the world, the world truth. This is the unknown physical factor, the missing link, that hinds the world of matter and force with the world of mind, the world of physics with the world of psychics, into a harmonious and related unity of the world truth.

in a circle, but water and earth downwards: but of those which revolve in a circle, the inerratic sphere commences its motion from the east, but the seven planets are carried in their orbits from the west. But of this there are many causes, among which the following is not the least: that if there was but one rapid period of the orbs, generation would be imperfect: but since there is a diversity of motion, it is also requisite that there should be a difference in the nature of bodies. It is, besides this, necessary that a celestial body should neither burn nor produce cold, nor generate any thing else which is the property of the four elements. But since **the world is a sphere,** which the zodiac evinces, and in every sphere the interior part is the middle, for it is every way much distant from the surface; hence heavy bodies are impelled downwards, and are driven to the earth: and all these indeed the gods fabricate, intellect orderly disposes, and soul perpetually moves. And thus much concerning the gods.

But there is a certain power subordinate to essence, but prior to soul; from essence indeed deriving its being, but perfecting soul, in the same manner as the sun perfects corporeal fight. And of souls some are rational and immortal, but others irrational and mortal; and the first of these are produced from the first, but the second from the second orders of Gods. But, in the first place, let us investigate the definition of soul. Soul then is that by which animated natures differ from such as are inanimate; but they differ through motion, sense, phantasy, and intelligence. The irrational

Unknown – *The History of Philosophy, Containing Those on whom the Attribute of Wise was Conferred* (1656)

CHAP. V.

Of the World.

Of matter was made *the World*. The World hath severall appellations, *the World, the All, the Whole*. World, is taken three waies: First, for God himselfe, who is properly qualified with all Essence, incorruptible, and ingenerate, who framed the Universe after a certain period of time; who resolved all nature into himselfe, and again generated it out of himselfe. Secondly for the stary Ornament: and thirdly that which consists of both.

The All is one way taken as faith, for the World, and another way for the System of the World, and the vacuity beyond it. The World is finite, the vacuity infinite.

Thus likewise they disinguish betwixt World and All: All includeth also an infinite vacuity in which the world is: World signifies the world without that vacuity, which neither is increased nor diminished; but its parts are sometimes extended, sometimes contracted. It began from the earth as its center, for the center is the beginning of a Circle.

The world is that which is properly qualified with the essence of all things; or, as *Chrysippus* and *Possidonius* define it, a System of Heaven and Earth, and of the nature therein contained; or a System of God and Men, and of all things that were made for them.

The world was made by God, for if (saith *Chrysippus*) there be any thing which produceth such things, as Man, though indued with reason, cannot produce, that (doubtlesse) is greater and stronger, and wiser then man. But a Man cannot make the Celestiall things, therefore that which made them, transcendeth man, in Art, Counsell, Prudence, and Power, and what can that be but God?

The World was made for those animate essences which have the use of Reason, these are the Gods and men, then whom nothing is better. All things of which it consisteth, and which it produceth within it selfe, are accommodated to the use of Man.

The World was made in this manner; God in the beginning being alone by himself, converted all substance (which according to *Zeno* was fire) first into air, then into Water. And is in the Plant the seed is contained; so God, who is the prolifick reason of the World, left such a seed in the humidity, as might afford easie and apt matter for the generation of those things that were to be produced.

Zeno addeth, that one part tending downward, was condensed into Earth, another part remained partly water, and partly, being exhal'd, air, of a particle of which air flashed out fire.

Cleanthes describeth it in this manner. The Universe being set on fire, the middle part thereof first setled downwards, then the next parts by little and little were quenched. Thus the Universe being wet, the extream fire, (the middle part opposing it) sprang upward, and began the constitution of the World, and the revolution of this constitution shall never end. For as the parts of every thing are at certain times produced of Seed; so the parts of the Universe (amongst which are living Creatures and Plants) are produced in their seasons; and as some reasons of the parts are mixed together in the feed, which being composed, are again dissolved, so of one are all things made; and again, of one is all compounded by an equall and perpetuall revolution.

The world is *One* of the same corporeall substance, and of a Sphæreical figure, for this is of all figures most apt for motion. Thus *Zeno, Chrysippus, Possidonius*, and others.

The World is reared in an infinite incorporeall vacuity, which is beyond it, circumsused about it, into which the world shall be dissolved by conflagration. The World is finite, the vacuity infinite, yet *Possidonius* faith, it is no more then will suffice for the revolution of the World, when it shall perish. By this argument they confute the motion of Atomes downward; introduced by *Epicure*, for in that which is infinite, there are no locall differences of high or low.

The world is not heavy, because the whole fabric thereof consisteth of heavy and light Elements, and, being placed in the midst, whither such bodies tend, it keepeth its place.

In the World there is no vacuity, but it is compleatly one, for that necessitates a conspiration and armony, betwixt Celestialls and Terrestrialls.

The World only is self-sufficient, because it alone hath all in it self, whereof it standeth in no need. Of it self it is nourished and augmented, whereas the parts are transmuted and converted into one another.

The World is a perfect body, the parts of the World are not perfect, because they are respective to the whole, and not of themselves. The Universe is by Nature apt to move it self in all parts, to contain, preserve, and not break, dissolve and burn it self, the Universe sending and moving the same point, and the parts thereof having the same motion from the Nature of the body. Like it is that this first motion is naturally proper to all Bodies, namely, to encline towards the midst of the World, considering the World moveth so in regard of it self; and the parts likewise, in that they are parts of the whole.

The World is a living Creature, rationall, animate and intellectual (so *Chrysippus, Apollodorus,* and *Possidonius*) and hath an animate sensible essence. For a living Creature is more excellent then at which is not a living Creature; but nothing is more excellent then the World, therefore the World is a living Creature. That it is animate is manifest from our Soul, which is a piece thereof taken out of it. (but *Boëthius* denies that the world is a living Creature) The mind, or Providence passeth through every part thereof, as the Soul doth in us, but in some parts more, in others lesse; through some permeating, as a habit, as in the bones and Nerves, through some as a mind, as through the principall (Hegemonick) part. In like manner the whole World is an animate rationall Creature, the Hegemonicall part thereof is the Æther, as *Antipater* the Tyrian, in his eighth Book of the World. But *Chrysippus* in his first of *Providence*, and *Possidonius*, *of the Gods*, affirm, that Heaven is the Hegemonick of the World; *Cleanthes*, the Sunne. But *Chrysippus* in the same Book (differing from what he said before) affirmeth it to be the purest part of the Æther, which they call the first God, sensibly, because it passeth through all in the air, and through all living Creatures and Plants, but through the Earth as a habit.

The World, according to the greater part of Stoicks, is corruptible, for it is generated in the same manner as things comprehensible by sense. Again, if the parts thereof be corruptible, the whole is also corruptible; but the parts of the World are corruptible, for they are dayly changed into one another, therefore the whole it selse is corruptible. And again, if any thing admit any change in the worse, it is corruptible; but the World doth, for it admitteth exsiccation, and inundation; therefore, *&c.*

The World shall perish by fire, caused by the power of fire which is in all things, which, after a long time, consuming all the moisture, shall resolve all things into it self. The Moon, Stars, and Sun, saith *Cleanthes*, shall perish, but God shall assimilate all things to himself, and resolve all into himself. This opinion of the general conflagration of the World, was held by the first and most antient of this sect, *Zeno, Cleanthes* and *Chrysippus*.

This fire is the Seed of the World; after the conflagration it diffuseth it self even into the Vacuity that was beyond the World. Afterwards, by order of the same reason which made the World, it shall withdraw and contract it self towards the generation of a new World, yet not be quite extinguished, but so as that some portion thereof remain, for as much as it is the cause of motion.

But *Boëthius, Possidonius,* and *Panœtius* deny this conflagration, of the World, conceiving rather that **the World is eternall**, to whom likewise *Diogenes* the Babylonian assents.

CHAP. VI.

Of Elements.

God having converted, as we said, all matter into moisture, and prepared it for the generation of future things, in the next place,

Sir Matthew Hale – *The Primitive Origination of Mankind: Considered and Examined According to the Light of Nature* (1677)

CHAP. III

A brief Consideration of the Hypotheses *that concern the Eternity of the World.*

[...]

And thus having considered these various suppositions touching the divers qualities or qualifications of this eternal Existence of the World, I shall now consider the subject Matter which men would thus have to be eternal, or at least possible to be such, namely the World. And herein even many of the assertors of the Eternity of the World, or the possibility thereof, have (and not without cause) faln into divers conclusions.

By the World therefore we must understand either the Matter of the World simply in it self, without being determined to this determinate Fabrick wherein it is; and thus it should seem that all those ancient Philosophers that have asserted the Eternity of the World, as *Aristotle*, and before him *Otellus Lucanus*: or, that have asserted *novitatem mundi in hac constitutione*, have agree; thus *Epicurus*, that asserts the coalition of Atoms into this Fabrick that we see, was of later edition than Eternity, yet asserts that these Atoms were eternal: and those Ancients mentioned by *Aristotle* in the 8th of his *Physicks*, that held that the World was made, and unmade and made again by eternal vicissitudes of *Amor & Inimicitia*, yet held the consituent Matter thereof eternal. And this seems to be the most comprehensive acceptation of the World.

2. Again, by the World we may understand the World as it is

now framed, the visisible World in that form and constitution as it now is; And thus it seems, *Aristotle* and those others that hold it proceeds necessarily from God as a necessary cause, or as a cause determined by his intrinsick Goodness, have held the World to be eternal; but yet we must not rest here. The world is like a goodly Palace, a fair large Building; but as in such a Palace there is first the case or fabric or *moles* of the Structure in it self, and besides that there are certain additaments that contribute to its ornament and use; as various Furniture, rare Fountains and Aqueducts, curious Motions of divers things appendicated to it, as Clocks, Engins, *&c.* so in the Goodly Universe there are the great Structure it self, and its great integrals the Heavenly and Elementary Bodies, framed in such a position and situation, the great Sceleton, as I may call it, of the World: But besides this there are very various and curious furnitures and accomodations of the Universe, as for instance, in our inferior World various Animals, Vegetables, Meteors, Minerals, Mixtures, and Men; and in the Heavenly Bodies various Motions and Aspects.

Now it will be necessary for him that asserts the Eternity of the World as it now stands, or the possibility of such an eternity, to consider whether he applies his assertion to the whole World, as consisting not only of the greater integrals whereof it consists, as the Heavenly and possibly the Elementary Bodies; but also of that furniture thereof consisting of Men, Animals, Vegetables, Meteors, Minerals, and those accomodations that are to it, as the Motions of the Heavenly Bodies; or whether he intends only some parts of it which seem more capable of an eternal existence, as being more fixed, and in themselves permanent, and so more able to sustain an eternal and consequently an immutable existence.

And upon examination we shall find either of these choices full of incurable difficulties, if not utter impossibilities, in relation to an eternal existence of the World or any parts thereof.

And this I shall in the order of this Discourse evince against all those former suppositions of Eternity; namely, 1. Against those that assert an independent eternal existence of the World: 2. Against those that assert an eternal but dependent existence thereof upon Almighty God, as a meer natural and necessary Cause thereof: 3. Against those that assert an eternal existence of the World dependent upon God as a free intellectual and voluntary Agent, but yet determined in his external emanations by the necessity of the Goodness and Beneficence of his nature: 4. Against those that assert at least a possibility of an eternal existence of the World, but dependent upon the freedom of the Divine Will undetermined by the necessity of his Beneficence.

First therefore concerning the supposition of the Eternity of the World in general; I shall not in this place dispute whether there be an utter impossibility of any material Being to be either independently or dependently eternal; enough may be said against it from the incapacity of any material Being to sustain such a kind of duration *à parte ante*, and yet without any derogation to the Divine Omnipotence or Goodness, which though infinite, yet cannot communicate such a duration to that which in its own intrinsick nature is not capable of it: Nor secondly, shall I dispute whether there be any such material or corporeal Being or Beings within the compass of the Universe, that hath or may have such or may have such a kind of permanence or fixedness in being that may be capable of an eternal existence *à parte ante*, either dependently or independently upon Almighty God; admitting by way of argument, but not granting it possible, that in the nature of the thing some material or corporeal Being may be of such a fixed, permanent consistence as may sustain such an eternal existence; and I here omit this dispute not because I make the least doubt of the beginning thereof by Creation, but because these are matters that require a longer and stricter process of enquiry and debate than I intend in this place: and therefore I shall descend to things that are more plain and evident, and yet such as will abundantly serve my design in the inquiry in hand.

And therefore for the present I shall *gratia argumenti* admit or suppose, 1. That there are or may be some corporeal things in the compass of the Universe that may possibly be of such a fixedness, stability and permanent nature that may sustain an eternal existence, at least dependently upon the supreme Cause. 2. And that possibly Matter it self undetermined to any particular form, or under any particular constitution; the Heavenly Bodies, the Elementary Bodies, and such as seem to have a simple nature; and possibly their figure, position, and situation may be such as might have this eternal existence, as the Sun, the Stars, the *Æther*, the four Elements; we will, for avoiding dispute touching it for the present, admit them to have been, or that possibly they might have been of that nature, quality, distance each from other eternally as now they are, like the great integrals and contignations, figure and concamerations of a goodly Palace: These things I say, though in themselves most certainly untrue, I shall for avoidance of difficult disputes admit at present. Yet I farther say, that though all these things were admitted, yet there are some great and considerable parts and integrals, and appendications unto the *Mundus aspectabilis that we* see, that are purely impossible to be eternal, and do *de facto* appear so to be; and consequently it is apparent that **the World in its full latitude and comprehension cannot be eternal.**

[...]

These things constituted and being in that state we find them, cannot without a total alteration of their nature and being from whatin truth they are, nor in the state of nature wherein they are placed, can they be eternal or without beginning: And these are very considerable and momentous parts or appendices of the World, and if it had been eternally without these, it had been a very lame and defective World, and such as the wisest man under Heaven could hardly understand for what use it would be, or why it should have continued in such a defective condition from the endless period of Eternity: Or at least if it had its use and beauty, certainly it had not had the same use that now it hath, nor the same beauty that now it hath.

And the consequence thereof is of great momentand importance, *viz.* **If these great accessions to the World, whereof I am speaking, could not be eternal, and yet without them the World would have been greatly deficient from what it is**, the greatest Arguments for the Eternity of the rest of the World will necessarily

CONCORDANCE

INDEX OF AUTHORS

33768569R00094

Made in the USA
Middletown, DE
26 July 2016